Volume 28

POVERTY, FOOD INSECURITY AND COMMERCIALIZATION IN RURAL CHINA

POVERTY, FOOD INSECURITY AND COMMERCIALIZATION IN RURAL CHINA

ZHONG TONG

Routledge
Taylor & Francis Group

LONDON AND NEW YORK

First published in 1993 by the University of Guelph

This edition first published in 2019
by Routledge
2 Park Square, Milton Park, Abingdon, Oxon OX14 4RN

and by Routledge
52 Vanderbilt Avenue, New York, NY 10017

Routledge is an imprint of the Taylor & Francis Group, an informa business

British Library Cataloguing in Publication Data
A catalogue record for this book is available from the British Library

ISBN: 978-1-138-48274-6 (Set)
ISBN: 978-0-429-42825-8 (Set) (ebk)
ISBN: 978-1-138-36899-6 (Volume 28) (hbk)
ISBN: 978-0-429-42890-6 (Volume 28) (ebk)

Publisher's Note
The publisher has gone to great lengths to ensure the quality of this reprint but
points out that some imperfections in the original copies may be apparent.

Disclaimer
The publisher has made every effort to trace copyright holders and would welcome
correspondence from those they have been unable to trace.

POVERTY, FOOD INSECURITY AND COMMERCIALIZATION

IN RURAL CHINA

by

ZHONG TONG

ABSTRACT

POVERTY, FOOD INSECURITY AND COMMERCIALIZATION
IN RURAL CHINA

Zhong Tong   Advisor:
University of Guelph, 1993   Professor Wayne Howard

This study analyzes the relationship among poverty, food insecurity, and
commercialization in rural China by employing agricultural household models. Data
are derived from a 10,000 household subsample of the annual rural household
consumption and expenditure survey.

In general, rural China appears to have no serious food insecurity issue,
primarily because land is equally distributed. Groups which are identified as "food
insecure" from sample data are not poor in income, and behave more as if they have
strong preferences for producing and/or consuming commodities other than food.

The results of econometric models of rural household supply and demand
for staple food show that both own-price and cross-price elasticities of marketed
surplus of grains are high, and in both affluent and poor areas. However, among low
income groups, the profit effect is sufficient to turn the own-price elasticity negative.

Overall increases in market prices of food should result in significant
increases in marketed surplus. However, government only controls quota amounts
and prices, and if it promotes commercialization by increasing quota prices or
eliminating quota procurement requirements, marketed surplus is likely to decline
sharply.

ACKNOWLEDGEMENT

I would like to express great appreciation to the International Food Policy Research Institute (IFPRI) for offering a wonderful research facility and generous assistance. I am grateful to my colleagues, Josh Rozen, Nicos Perez, Joachim von Braun, Tricia Klosky, and Jane He for providing exceptional help.

I thank my supervisor, Professor Wayne Howard, for his patient supervision, and Professor Erna van Duran, whose advice and organization was so helpful. I am also very grateful to all committee members, besides Professor van Duran and Howard, Professor Kokchiang Tan and Professor Truman Phillips, for their encouragement and helps at the last stage.

Finally, I am indebted to my husband, Tom Wiens, without whose financial support, emotional encouragement, and generous help, this thesis would have taken longer to reach fruition.

Table of Contents

iv

List of Tables

List of Figures

I. INTRODUCTION

The Chinese government, for over a decade, has been carrying out rural economic reforms by employing a policy of decreased control over production, market activities, and income distribution in order to provide an incentive structure favouring increased production, and especially commercial production in the rural areas. This has been generally successful in raising incomes and solving the food insecurity problem in most areas. However, certain groups have been left behind in the general progress -- the inhabitants of poor regions and perhaps also the most impoverished portion of the rural community within the more advanced regions. In 1985, there were 102 million rural poor, or was ten percent of the total population, and the extreme poor were 40 million (OLGEDPA, 1989).

Prior to 1985, the government has dealt with this "poverty problem" by providing special subsidies or relief ("Blood transfusion"), but the gap in incomes has continued to grow and is politically embarrassing for a "socialist" government. The poverty problem touches some especially sensitive nerves, as many of the poverty areas are also "old revolutionary base areas", a wellspring of support for the revolution, while others are inhabited by minority peoples whose relationship with the Han (Chinese majority) dominated government has long been problematic. Some of these latter are border areas where the political support of the local population has strategic importance. In response, the government has begun to change its approach, moving from "blood transfusion" to "blood making", by providing increasing amounts of investment assistance (including infrastructure improvement) in the hope of raising productivity. It also seeks to expand the scope of commercial production in the poverty areas, in the belief that only by moving away from a subsistence orientation is there hope that the poor may escape permanently from poverty.

Poverty is often reflected in a combination of low incomes and inadequate food consumption. Therefore, poverty alleviation policy commonly addresses the issue of food security. In doing so, the temptation is to focus on farm self-sufficiency as a goal, to the exclusion of commercialized approaches to food supply. If the government exercises administrative control over farming, it can direct the majority of resources to food production, force a subsistence orientation, and/or develop a rationing system to equalize food consumption regardless of income. If the government avoids direct administrative controls, it can mainly influence relative prices, leaving individual farmers to decide how much to sell and how much to consume. **In such a market-driven farming system, the question remains whether, with growth of commercial production, market forces will largely solve the food security problems of the poor, or whether special administrative measures need be taken to address food security problems?**

Food security for the whole population was one of the major goals of the Chinese government in constructing "socialist" China -- a goal for which great efforts were exerted. The government adopted food self-sufficiency as its general food security policy. To increase the overall availability (production) and guarantee food access to the whole population were the two main concerns. Land reform (lasting several years from 1949) tended to equalize the resources available to all farmers and, by abolishing rents, to enable food self-sufficiency (Walker, 1984). The policy of "Unified Procurement and Sale" (implemented after 1953) guaranteed low-priced ration grain to urban residents, and reliable marketing at completely stable prices to farmers (i.e., no market risk) (Walker, 1984). Collectivisation (from cooperatives in 1955-57 to communes in 1958-83) reduced disparity in household resources and ensured virtually equal food consumption regardless of effort or wealth (Barnett, 1979).

Poverty reduction can be called another major objective of the formation of agricultural producers' cooperatives and the people's communes in the 1950s. However, the levelling of wealth which resulted, while contributing to food security and equalizing the income distribution within particular accounting units, did not greatly increase the living standard of the poor. Collectivization could not extinguish the remaining sources of poverty, due to geographic differences in endowments among accounting units and disparities in labor endowment among families. The latter were dealt with to a limited extent by maintaining small local and national relief funds to assist the elderly and dependents of living or dead soldiers.

At the same time, a number of policies, including some of those mentioned above, also aimed at facilitating extraction of an agricultural surplus, tended to impoverish farmers, and often were especially harmful to the poor. Restrictions on labor markets and migration associated with collectivization trapped the poor on unproductive farmlands. Tight controls over cropping decisions and procurement quotas, together with restrictions on income-earning activities in the countryside, kept rural inhabitants excessively focused on grain production, regardless of comparative advantage. State control of agricultural prices reduced farm profitability.

Although the government's economic reforms in the early 1980s were not specifically targeted on the poor, they did seek to raise farmers' living standards. The major reforms were of general benefit to all farmers; however, some policies at least initially targeted poverty areas. For example, the return to family farming, under the "Production Responsibility System" (PRS), was initiated locally in poverty areas where collective farming had clearly not benefitted the rural population. It was first officially extended to the poorest one-third of counties; and not until 1983 was de-collectivization sanctioned as nationwide policy. But it is also arguable that poverty areas did not benefit much from the new freedom to engage in non-farm occupations, when this policy was extended to encourage collective investment in rural industries, as only the wealthier collectives had much capital to invest.

Consequently, some rural areas which at the time seemed relatively impoverished made rapid advances in the early 1980s, whereas other poverty areas seemed to remain stagnant. This was reflected in provincial statistics for real growth of gross value of agricultural production during 1979-82, when, for example, Anhui, Sichuan, Guizhou, Guangxi (relatively poor provinces) grew rapidly (18-27%), but

Gansu, Qinghai, Shaanxi, and Ningxia (as poor or worse) grew extremely slowly (0-8%) (World Bank, 1985).

The "poor areas" which were able to escape extreme poverty as a result of the initial policy reforms were generally those where the geographical or physical endowment was favorable, but previous policies had suppressed opportunities for profitable activities. These included areas which had been forced to devote most of their land to grain through high procurement quotas, despite comparative advantage in cash crops or livestock; areas with considerable labor surpluses and easy access to urban centres; and areas where traditions of handicrafts or commerce had been well-developed but suppressed in recent years.

On the other hand, most of the remaining poverty areas -- those which remained on the official "poor counties" list in 1986 (691 counties)-- included those poorly-endowed by geographic location (remote and mountainous) and at a disadvantage in agricultural resources (soil, rainfall, climate, etc.). Many of these areas suffered from severe ecological dagradation (deforestation, soil erosion, etc.) Infrastructure, particularly transport links with the outside, was lacking. For example, in Sichuan Province, there were still 50% of villages without motor-road access in 1986, within the "poor counties" there were 16.1% of township lacked road access (OLGEDPA, 1989).

All these disadvantages in natural endowment and rural infrastructure made it impossible for the poor areas to keep up with the pace of other areas in developing commercialization. A general examination of provincial statistics on the extent of agricultural commercialization during 1983-88 suggests some of the issues which need further study.[1] These data show that agricultural commercialization (sales divided by total agricultural product) increased in every area during the 1980s, from an average of 34% in 1983 to 51% in 1988. There were, however, considerable regional differences in commercial rates which, in 1983, ranged from 17% to 49% among provinces; and in 1988 ranged from 41% to 75% (CAYEC, 1990).

This study will explore the relationships among the three phenomena described above -- poverty, commercialization, and food insecurity in China and specifically test (1) whether food insecurity is still a major characteristic of the poor, and (2) whether commercialization is positively correlated with income and food security (or whether the poor concentrate on food production and are less commercialized due to a concern of food security).

Poverty, defined in terms of low levels of income, is often, but not always associated with chronic or temporary inadequacy of diet -- that is, food insecurity. Commercialization -- a process involving decreasing self-sufficiency and increased

---

[1] The data used here compare sales of agricultural products with gross agricultural income, where the latter includes self-consumption. Sales were valued at actual procurement or market prices (rising rapidly during the period), self-consumption at quota procurement prices (relatively stable). To distinguish "real" increase in commercialization from the differential impact of price escalation, it was necessary to deflate sales and self-consumption using separate price indices, to measure each in constant (1983) prices. Moreover, the statistical definition of gross agricultural income was changed in 1985, when the value of output of village industry was re-assigned to industrial product. For the sake of consistency, 1983-84 gross agricultural income in each province was approximately adjusted to the post-1984 definition. Thus two sources of bias which give an exaggerated impression of the rate at which commercialization was proceeding have been removed.

participation in the market -- is not normally thought to be associated with poverty, but rather with escape from poverty.

In analyzing the relationship among poverty, food insecurity and commercialization -- mainly the impact of poverty and food insecurity on commercialization -- agricultural household models are employed as the framework for theoretical analysis. These models are applied empirically to test these relationships using sub-provincial data (county data for 1983-87 collected by International Food Policy Research Institute and household data for 1988 collected by the University of California-Riverside and the Chinese Academy of Social Sciences (**UCR-CASS**)). Based on the results, appropriate policies for alleviation of poverty and food insecurity will be suggested.

The study is divided into four parts. The first part contains a discussion on the concepts of relationships among poverty, commercialization, and food insecurity, including concepts and definitions, a literature review, and previous studies on the agricultural household models. The second part contains a historical review of the Chinese government's policies dealing with poverty, commercialization, and food insecurity. The third contains Chinese agricultural household models, and listing of testable hypotheses. The fourth part discusses the statistics and econometric analysis of the household data set, and empirical results. The last part summarizes the conclusions and policy implications.

II. THEORETICAL INSIGHT INTO THE POVERTY, FOOD SECURITY AND COMMERCIALIZATION NEXUS

A. Concepts and Definition

Proper definition of the three concepts of poverty, commercialization, and food security is a crucial step in translating policy issues to research problems. In the development literature, **commercialization** is defined as a transition process from subsistence agriculture to commercial agriculture (or from an autarkic economy to a market economy) (Wharton, 1968). However, **as used in this study, it means an increase in the extent of production for market sale or dependence on the market**. Such an increase may be promoted by government through various policy instruments, such as investments in infrastructure which reduced marketing costs or losses; reduction or removal of policy restrictions on marketing; or intervention (or reduction of intervention) in the price system, such as by eliminating administered prices or subsidies.

With this definition, **it should be clear that "commercialization" is not in itself a policy instrument, nor is it an independent variable -- rather it is an outcome, or dependent variable, of farmer decision-making**. Strictly speaking, one can ask whether commercialization is empirically associated with reduced poverty or increased food security, but not whether commercialization "alleviates" poverty. To look at cause and effect relationships, it is more useful to focus on the specific policy instruments (e.g., price interventions or investments) as purely causative factors, treating commercialization, along with poverty reduction and food security, as joint effects.

There are three alternative ways to measure commercialization: (a) gross sales (income) as a proportion of total production value (gross income); (b) net cash income as a proportion of total net income; and (c) cash purchases as a proportion of total consumption. Usually (a) and (b) will differ because the division of production costs into cash and self-supplied components will not be in the same proportion as sales occupy in total production. If savings are absent, (b) = (c), e.g., all cash earning equals cash purchasing. In the context of household models (and ignoring savings/dissavings and external income sources), sales determines cash income, which determines cash purchases, so the three measures will vary together.

Poverty must be defined in terms of failure of individuals or families to meet some standard of adequate livelihood, which may be relative or absolute. Absolute poverty, for the farm household, has been defined in China as (1) lacking capacity for savings or investment, hardly having enough to meet working capital requirements; and (2) not obtaining sufficient income to meet the minimum requirement for survival (Jiang, 1990). The survival standard may involve a specific "basket" of essential consumption goods and services, or a monetary measure of total income or consumption. "Food" would certainly be a big part of any essential consumption basket, and if being poor were defined only as lacking food, then it would not be possible to distinguish conceptually between poverty and food insecurity. We wish to maintain the conceptual distinction, or we may ask whether the poor must also fall into food insecurity. A more appropriate definition of poverty for our purposes is based on the monetary level of income or aggregate consumption.

There are many ways to <u>measure the degree of poverty</u> or to define a poverty line. The common characteristic of poverty, however, is that the standard of living does not reach a level regarded as tolerable by society. The tolerable standard of living can be defined either in terms of minimum human survival needs, or as a degree of quality of life. Both definitions concern consumption of goods and services, so that expenditure would be an appropriate indicator of consumption.

Measures of relative poverty are essentially arbitrary. The usual approach is to take the lowest quintile or decile of the population on income or consumption to be "the poor." However, income and consumption may not be equal or consistent at any particular time (with gaps covered by borrowing or other transfers), and it is unclear which is the more consistent indicator of poverty status.

Food security has been defined as access by all people at all times to enough food for an active, healthy life (Reutlinger, 1987). This requires both <u>overall availability</u> of food and <u>ability to acquire it</u> <u>at all times</u>. Conversely, food insecurity is the lack of access to sufficient food, either chronically or transitorily and leads to poor health, reduced energy, stunting, etc.. <u>Chronic</u> food insecurity is due to unavailability of food or lack of resources to acquire it. <u>Transitory</u> food insecurity is a temporary decline in a household's access to food, due to instability in food <u>production</u>, <u>prices or market availability</u>, or <u>household incomes</u>.

A more refined examination of the concept of "sufficient food" requires consideration of nutritional status, as not only the quantity but the types and quality of food may be relevant issues, and sufficient quantity but inadequate nutritional composition may have the same adverse consequences as insufficient quantity (i.e., lack of an active healthy life).

Food security is also sometimes equated with food self-sufficiency, either by household or national availability. Clearly if trade is possible, food self-sufficiency is not a prerequisite to food security. But, as implied above, in the absence of food self-sufficiency, food security requires some combination of stability in overall food availability, prices, and incomes (or ability to buy food), again either or both at the household and national level.

There is no single measure of the status of food security. The appropriate measure depends on the level of aggregation at which the problem is analyzed and the availability of statistics. Typically, low levels of food consumption and/or high interhousehold, intrahousehold, or intertemporal variation in food consumption (especially at low consumption levels) are taken as indicators of food insecurity. If low food consumption is not compelled by circumstances, but is voluntary, it does not indicate food insecurity, however. Food consumption is measured in terms of nutritional intake, often broken down into measures of energy, protein, and lipids (fat). Recent research findings (Cornell) suggest that energy is by far the most crucial measure, because varied diets which supply sufficient energy are likely to supply adequate protein, and no required minimum level of lipid intake can be specified.

B. Literature Review

Food security, poverty, and commercialization have been subjects of interest to many researchers. Studies on food security commonly focus on the definition and measurement of food insecurity, and on government policies and programs dealing with this issue. The studies on poverty mainly concern determination of the poverty line, and evaluation of the impact of government policies on poverty. The majority of the studies on commercialization focus on impacts of commercialization on income, food security, and nutritional status. A few studies were of the impact of poverty and food security concerns on the marketed surplus, taken as a proxy of commercialization. Since growth of cash cropping is often considered the essence of commercialization, many studies have dealt with the factors, such as farm size or land ownership, which influence decision making on resource allocation between subsistence crops and cash crops.

This section will review the previous studies on (1) measurement and causes of food insecurity, (2) food insecurity and poverty, and (3) relationship among poverty, food security and commercialization.

1. Food Security and Causes and Measurement of Food Insecurity

Food security is one of the major issues of concern to most developing countries' governments. Food security refers to the availability of and access to food.

Any risk associated with either would cause food insecurity (von Braun et al., 1992).

The major causes of food insecurity, which vary from country to country, range from

failure of macroeconomic policies, to an economic and political structure of local

societies that suppresses the acquisition of sufficient food by many households. Food

insecurity may be chronic or transitory (Reutlinger, 1987). Chronic food insecurity

is caused by the lack of continuous access to food, due either to shortfalls of

production or purchasing power, and cannot be relieved by temporary assistance.

Transitory food insecurity is caused by unexpected events, such as bad harvests

resulting from natural disaster, or price and income instability due to policy change,

and can be relieved by temporary approaches. Famine is the worst manifestation of

transitory food insecurity, and poverty is the root cause of chronic food insecurity

Food availability of households is determined by (or relies on) the national or local

food supply. However, at national, regional and community levels, fluctuations in

food production, stockholding and trade may cause corresponding fluctuations in food

availability (von Braun et. al., 1992) . Seasonal variations in price, or sudden changes

in income and price may also result in food shortage (Sahn and von Braun, 1987).

However, there is no single indicator commonly used to measure food

insecurity. At the national level, food insecurity can be monitored through food

demand and supply, stock and trade. At the household level, it can be monitored by

direct indicators -- food consumption and nutrition information. Other

socioeconomic indicators, such as real wage rates, price levels, employment, and anthropometric status, can complement this monitoring (Haddad, Sullivan and Kennedy, 1991 and Beaton et. al., 1992).

Existence of food insecurity will lead to reduction of household labor productivity due to malnutrition and illness, and misallocation of scarce resources since the households attempt to combat food shortage in the short-run by selling off productive assets (von Braun et al., 1992). In addition, some actions resulting from food insecurity are associated with environmental degradation (Leonard and contributors, 1989): for example, most food-insecure households live in ecologically vulnerable areas, with low land productivity (e.g., in China's poor areas), and in order to solve temporary food insufficient problem, reclaim land by clearing forest, leading to further deterioration of the ecological system (Jiang et. al., 1989).

2. Who and Where are the Food Insecure?

The poor, especially in low-income countries, are presumed to be the most food-insecure group of people. In other words, food insecurity is a central characteristic of poverty. However, it is difficult to indicate the exact number of food-insecure poor since estimation bases differ. Generally, food-deficient households are considered food insecure, but some households frequently move into and or out of the category of food-deficiency. Based on malnutritional status, the FAO estimated that for 1983-1985, there were 512 million undernourished at the 1.4

basal metabolic rate (BMR)[2], and the World Bank estimated that 730 million people did not have sufficient income to obtain food to maintain a healthy life in 1980s (World Bank, 1990). The International Food Research Institute (IFRI) (Broca and Orem, 1991) estimated that about 595 million people were calorie-deficient, excluding China, where there were about 40 million extreme poor, who did not have secure access to food (OLGEDPA, 1989). A recent World Bank report indicated that a considerable reduction in the incidence of poverty has taken place in recent years (World Bank, 1993). However, other estimates suggest that the numbers of food-insecure people have increased due to rapid population growth, especially in Sub-Saharan Africa (von Braun et al., 1992).

Food-insecure people are characterized as being under severe constraints either from failure of their own production, which is not able to provide sufficient food for all household members, or from lack of access to the market to purchase their food due to low income. In general, they lack "exchange entitlement" (Sen, 1982). These poor are usually landless or smallholders, who are the most vulnerable group in society and the most injured from economic and political shocks. The finding from 13 survey areas in Africa, Asia, and Latin America on income sources of the malnourished rural poor (von Braun and Pandya-Lorch, 1991) has shown (i) family size and composition are positively correlated with food insecurity, and the

---

[2] Basal metabolic rate (BMR) is the indicator to measure energy and protein expenditure to maintain the basic body needs for normal activities. BMR is determined principally by body size, body composition, and age. Sex and body weight also contribute to BMR. BMR for girls to maintain normal or light activity is 1.5, for boys is 1.6 (WHO. 1985).

higher the dependency rate and younger the composition of families, the more serious is food insecurity; (ii) ownership of land for farming is a major source of food security -- landless or semi-landless households are at higher risk; (iii) food security is related to who controls income, since female household heads spend a higher percentage of income on food; and (iv) no general statement can be made as to whether income diversification has positive or negative effects on food security, as it depends on location specific factors.

3. Poverty and Food Insecurity

Policies and programs for improving chronic food insecurity are always associated with policies for poverty alleviation at the household level. The most effective long-run strategy is to build up the poor households' capacity to rise above their poverty status and thereby enhance their ability to combat food insecurity. Production-oriented policies and programs are one appropriate means for this objective. These policies and programs encourage farmers to intensify production of staple food for own-consumption or cash sale. Technological innovation enables the increase in production and commercialization brings more employment opportunity, thus increasing income (von Braun et al., 1992).

Another approach to poverty alleviation is direct targeting of employment generation and income increase. Examples of relevant programs include labor-intensive public works and credit for consumption stabilization and self-employment (von Braun et al., 1992). Labor-intensive public works programs deal with three related issues -- food insecurity, growing unemployment and poor infrastructure prevailing in most developing countries. In the short run, the programs bring the poor a "windfall profit" (Kumar and Chowhuri, 1985), while in the long run the programs, such as the Employment Guarantee Schedule (EGS) in Maharashtra, India, can increase the poor's resistance to famine (Ezekiel and Stuyt, 1989). Credit for consumption stabilization and self-employment serves to promote growth and diversification of rural economies. The most successful programs of this type have occurred in the relatively well-developed areas where rural infrastructure is good and market activity is vigorous (von Braun et al., 1992).

Direct income transfer programs can be made either through food distribution or food subsidy to needy groups. Targeted feeding programs are aimed at the most vulnerable malnutrition group -- children and women of child-bearing age of low income. School feeding programs not only provide food to children, but also have a social impact by encouraging parents to send their children to school. Food stamps are a means of implementing a welfare transfer program for low-income groups. However, the administrative problems, such as identifying the needy group, detracts from the original objective, to stimulate higher food consumption and reach the poorest people (Edirisinghe, 1987).

Unlike food stamps, food price subsidies are applicable to the entire population, not specific to a given group. Food price subsidies have provided a positive and significant service in improving household food security, especially food consumption of preschoolers, through public distribution. In practice, it is an income transfer program. Subsidized food, generally, has accounted for 15-25 percent of low-income households' real incomes. Consumer food price subsidy programs, which aim at assuring consumers of access to specified quantities of food at subsidized prices (Pinstrup-Andersen and Alderman, 1988), are very commonly employed in middle and low income countries. However, original objectives are ofted perverted by special interest groups' intervention, which expands the categories of subsidized food or subsidized consumers for their own benefit. Generalized price subsidies, which set lower market prices for a commodity such as staple food for some or all people of the community, are usually fiscally costly, and not very progressive in distribution of benefits. Rationing seems to be more effective than price subsidies; however, experience has shown that rationing alone is insufficient to reach both the goals of universal household food security and targeted income transfer (von Braun et al., 1992).

Food aid has a variety of functions, stabilizing the price of food, providing emergency relief and balance of payment support. In opposition to the general conclusion about food aid that it provided disincentives to domestic producers and caused misallocation of resources and dependency, the empirical evidence has shown its positive impact in some developing countries, as in India and South Korea, which used it to develop their own food production and no longer rely on food aid (Maxwell and Singer, 1979). Food aid can be properly used in developing countries's food policies. Currently food aid is increasingly used for developmental purposes, e.g., to finance local infrastructure construction (von Braun et al., 1992).

The distributional policies and programs mentioned above have sometimes failed to reach or benefit the targeted group, the poor. Besides external assistance, enhancing the poor's capacity to combat food insecurity is the real agenda. As it relates to the policies that encourage poor farmers to increase their production of staple foods or shift to cash crop production, commercialization is the proper term to define this process.

4. Commercialization in Developing Countries

Commercialization is regarded as the cornerstone of economic development in developing countries (Kennedy and Cogill, 1987). In many developing countries, commercialization has become an inevitable trend induced by urbanization, non-agricultural sector development in rural areas and technological change in agricultural production in recent decades (von Braun and Kennedy, 1986).

"Commercialization" is a transitional process leading away from subsistence agriculture. It can occur in different aspects, on the input side, output side, and in income sources through an increasing share of market transactions (von Braun, 1989). There is also a conceptual confusion, between commercialization of agriculture and commercialization of rural economy. The former refers to an increase in marketed surplus of agricultural products, whereas the latter refers to increased marketing of the products of the rural sector. The definition is also confused with its measurement (Sharif, 1986). To measure commercialization of farm households, an aggregate indicator would be the ratio of net marketed surplus to income. It is also noticeable that case studies use different measures depending on the aspect of the process of commercialization being discussed. For example, in the Philippines (Bouis and Haddad, 1990) and Kenya case studies (Kennedy and Cogill, 1987), farmers shifting from subsistence staple food production to sugarcane increased their proportion of market sales (output side); whereas in China since 1970 commercialization has been reflected in the growth of modern input utilization (input side) as well as market sales (Stone, 1988; RGCRDI, 1984).

The process of commercialization varies from country to country or region to region within the same country, depending on economic development, social conditions, and the traditional customs. Most typically, technological change and appropriate governmental sector policy result in an increase in staple food production (von Braun and Kennedy, 1986). Higher food productivity may result in staple food becoming a cash crop, or may induce a shift of land and labor to a cash crop which is entirely sold in the market. Another alternative stimulus to commercialization is the government's implementation of an export promotion policy, encouraging farmers to produce cash crops for export, and importing food in order to exploit comparative advantage or engage in trade arbitrage (von Braun et al., 1989).

Market integration, rural infrastructure improvement, and appropriate government policy are the essential facilitators of a transition from subsistence agriculture to commercialization (von Braun and Kennedy, 1986). Technology change in agriculture is the crucial factor in increasing productivity (land and labor), allowing labor to shift from staple food production to more labor-intensive cash crop production or to engagement in nonagricultural activities.

However, there are risks of crop production failure, price variation, and deterioration of marketing channels confronting farm households, especially smallholders, when cash crops are introduced (von Braun, Hotchkiss and Immenk, 1989). Smallholders have scarce land and other production assets, and allocate most resources to food crop production for food security's sake. However, farmers would switch to cash cropa only if it is more profitable than food cropping by an amount (risk premium) sufficient to offset increased risk (von Braun and Kennedy, 1986). Moreover, some case studies have shown food production increasing even as farmers grow more cash crops (von Braun and Kennedy, 1986), due to productivity increases, which reduce or eliminate food insecurity.

5. Relationship Among Poverty, Food Security and Commercialization

Studies on the relationship among poverty, food security and commercialization primarily relate to two aspects: (1) smallholder households' marketing behavior as related to wealth status and food security concerns; and (2) impact of commercialization on income and nutritional status.

Commercialization is referred to as a process of increasing marketed surplus (Hinderink and Sterkenburg. 1987). However, the distinction is made between two different types of commercializers: true and desperation (or distressed). The former is associated with surplus production of immediate family needs, while the latter is associated with a need for cash to provide subsistence (i.e., with low income families who are not self-sufficient yet still market produce) (Lele, 1987). Usually "desperation" commercialization is primarily associated with smallholders, who have poor resource endowment, while "true" commercialization is always carried out by large farms (Cohen, 1988). The "desperation" commercializers are low-income smallholders with extreme land pressure and food deficit. The cross-sectional relationship between marketing percentage and family income thus might be a U-cruve, e.g., as found in Malawi (Randolph, 1992).

Peasant households in developing countries devote a great proportion of their inputs (land and labor) to staple food crops. When production of such crops increases in response to price changes, households either sell (treating staple foods as cash crops) or consume the increased output. A number of early empirical studies (Bardhan, 1970, Toquero et. al, 1975, Haessel, 1975, Chinn, 1958) focussed on the issue of decisionmaking of grain-producing households. Most found the price elasticity of marketed surplus of grain (usually rice) to be positive, in Thailand (Behrman, 1966), Taiwan (Chinn, 1958), Philippines (Toquero et. al., 1975), and India (Haessel, 1975). Although price elasticities of consumption were also positive due to the income effect, the elasticity of marketed surplus was much larger than that of consumption; i.e., when production increases, the households sell a large proportion of increases and retain a small proportion for own consumption (Chinn, 1975, Haessel, 1975). However, Bardhan (1970) found that the price elasticity of marketed surplus of foodgrain in Indian was negative, although, using a different model, Haessel obtained the opposite result (Haessel, 1975).

Commercialization also refers to the shift from subsistence cropping to cash cropping at the household level, based on principles of comparative advantages (Matthews, 1988). Cash crops can be food crops or nonfood crops (von Braun and Kennedy, 1986). Introduction of cash crops is encouraged if producers have surplus food in a climatically-normal year (Bryceson, 1988), or by government policies which favor cash crop producers (Maxwell and Fernando, 1989). However, there will be competition in allocating resources (capital, land, and labor) between subsistence crop and cash crop. In developing countries, the majority of smallholder households lack capital, which is needed more for growing cash crops than subsistence crops (Maxwell, 1988). Scarcity of land is another constraint on shifting to cash crops. In Zomba district of Malawi, for example, the smallholders' marketed surplus of agricultural output was very low. This was because they primarily devoted their land to food production rather than cash crops due to the land pressure (Randolph, 1992). Therefore, the households would either produce enough food for own consumption and cash crop for cash or produce insufficient food and no cash crop (Whitehead, 1988).

"Safety first" was another consideration of these smallholders, who would face market risk from growing cash crops. For example, they usually protect against market risk by storing their food instead of selling it.

It is also argued by some that a U-curve describes the relationship between degree of commercialization and income among smallholder households. Although successful smallholders (relative well-off) generate most sales of food crops, the poorest may also sell their food crops, but due to desperate cash need, for items such as taxes, tuition, and consumer goods. If their income situation improves, they will continue to grow food for own consumption, but not for sales. This gives rise to a U-shaped commercialization and income relationship (Cohen, 1988). In studies of Nigeria, Ivory Coast, and Malawi, such a U-curve was found in cross-sectional data. But the Malawi study clarified that the low-incomed households with high commercialization mostly depended on off-farm income to survive: among households dependent mainly on farming for income, a positive relationship between commercialization and income was very clear (Randolph, 1992). Increasing access to agricultural resources, i.e., land, labor and capital, and proximity of marketing outlets raises marketed surplus of households.

The poor are usually risk averse, and face additional production risk with new and unfamiliar crops, as well as market risk. Market risk encompasses both cash crop price variation and food price variation, as farmers marketing cash crops would also need to purchase food in the market. "Subsistence-first" considerations would likely become their decision-making rule (Hammer, 1986) -- that is, farmers will keep a certain proportion of land in food no matter what. Maximizing profit by efficiently allocating resources is supposed to be the principle of farmers' decision-making. However, it is not always dominant when risk factors (production and market) are involved. "Safety-first" may be more dominant in smallholders' decision-making than pure maximization of profit (Shahabuddin and Mestelma, 1986) -- that is, farmers may protect themselves against risks before considering profitability.

6. The Impact of Commercialization on Income, Food Consumption and Nutritional Status

Previous studies have found inconsistent results on the impacts of commercialization (specifically, the introduction of cash crops) on income, food consumption and nutritional status. Inconsistencies (i.e., relationships suggesting different signs in different cases) have been found among studies (i) of countries growing cash crops, (ii) on the same country and with the same cash crop, (iii) of different cash crops in the same country (von Braun and Kennedy, 1986). Several factors are supposed to contribute to the inconsistencies: *different methodologies*, such as ex-post analysis employing cross-sectional data versus comparisons based on intertemporal data; *different underlying assumptions*, such as assuming intrahousehold income distribution is equitable when looking at the relationship between income and food consumption, while when dealing with intrahousehold food consumption this assumption has to be removed; *different data*, for example, used to estimate income elasticity of caloric consumption, when the distinction between caloric availability and caloric intake is a crucial one (Bouis and Haddad, 1992); and *different indicators* used to assess the results, especially single versus comprehensive indicators (von Braun and Kennedy, 1986).

It is still controversial whether commercialization brings benefits to all social groups, whether it increases the incomes of farmers who move from traditional subsistence agriculture to specialized cash crop cultivation; if it does, whether the increased income is spent on food or something else; and, if it improves food consumption, whether nutritional status of all members of households, especially women and children, is improved. von Braun and Kennedy have summarized nine studies for five countries done prior to 1983 which show mixed impacts on income, food consumption and nutritional status (von Braun and Kennedy, 1986).

Income gains from increasing commercialization *per se* may not materialize in case farmgate prices of export crops prove lower than anticipated due to unexpected taxes, falling world market prices, and/or exploitation of local monopsony power. An increase in input prices and long-run declines in productivity of export crops also may reduce returns to production of export crops (Pinstrup-Andersen and Garcia, 1983). The loss of returns (or rents) to the scarcest resource may contribute to unexpectedly low income gains. Land is usually the scarcest resource, but in Sub-Saharan Africa, seasonal labor is also counted as a constraint. Comparing the returns per unit of land, cash crops may prove higher than subsistence crops, but they also show higher variance of returns to scarce resources. Therefore it is necessary to take risk into account when evaluating returns to cash cropping.

When examining the effect of commercialization on incomes, nominal and real increases should be distinguished: usually an increase in nominal incomes results from sales for households which shift from subsistence to cash crops.

However, this does not necessarily mean an increase in real income. If the food crop market is localized, a reduction of food supply may push up food prices, offsetting nominal increases in income. An increase in the prices of other consumer goods would have the same consequence (von Braun and Kennedy, 1986).

Whether or not gains in income improve food consumption depends on the form in which income is received (as continuous or discontinuous flows), and on who controls income within the household (Kennedy and Cogill, 1987). Usually, semi-subsistence agriculture involves relatively continuous income flows, a high percentage of which are likely to be spent on food. Cash crop growers may receive discontinuous cash payments and spend a higher proportion on durable goods (von Braun, 1989). Female heads of households spend a greater portion of increased income on food than do male heads (Kennedy and Cogill, 1987).

C. The Agricultural Household Models

1. Introduction

Agricultural household models have been increasingly employed in research on the farmers' behaviour and choices in developing countries since 1980. Agriculture is the major sector in most developing countries' economies. The agricultural household is the major form of production unit in developing countries, although each country's political, economic and institutional system varies. The agricultural household models are used to provide relevant information about farmer decision making in production, consumption, and labor supply. The models also can be used to describe farmers' response to policy interventions (Singh, Squire, and Strauss, 1986, abbreviated *SSS*).

The pioneers who first estimated the empirical models of agricultural households in the 1970s included researchers at the Food Research Institute of Stanford University and at the World Bank. The early models were intended to facilitate econometric studies. For example, they normally employed the Cobb-Douglas production function, and simplified by aggregating demand into three variables -- one agricultural good produced and consumed by the household, one non-agricultural commodity purchased in the market, and leisure.

Since subsistence agriculture is still a dominant pattern in many developing countries, the process of decision-making may combine production, consumption and labor supply simultaneously. However, when the market, either input market or output market or both, exists and functions well, subsistence agriculture enters a transition to semisubsistence or commercial agriculture. The decision-making process has to assume that the market functions of input purchase, output sales and labor supply do not occur simultaneously. A simultaneous process of decision-making is replaced by a sequential or recursive process.

The agricultural household model is used to analyze the process of decision-making of farm households in order to derive the optimum results for the household in production (and marketed surplus), consumption of agricultural and non-agricultural commodities, and labor supply on farm and off farm (hired in and out). The optimum is defined as one, which maximizes utility (or expected utility) from consumption subject to various constraints, such as resource limitations (land, labor and capital), budget (expenditure equal to income), and government policy (e.g., procurement requirement). It is also very useful in examining the impact of changes in price (input or output or both), technology and policy on household's wealth, consumption and production.

Some of the earliest work with household models was designed to account for differences between the behaviour of the purely-competitive capitalist firm as predicted by neoclassical microeconomic theory and the observed behaviour of peasant farms in developing countries. Initial focus was on the presumed subsistence orientation of peasant producers (Wharton, 1968). It was noted that subsistence-oriented households are a combined body of producer and consumer. On the consumer side, the family members consume only what they produce, meaning that family utility was maximized through consumption of a bundle of goods (food and non-food) produced only within the household using family-owned resources: land, labor, and capital.

However, it had to be recognized that purely subsistence farms were really no more common in developing countries than pure commercial farms. Rather, semisubsistence family farms were the norm. These are engaged in mixed farm and non-farm production activities, and consume their own produce as well as buying and selling products in the market. Labor is not necessarily a fixed factor of production, but is hired in and out. Explanations of the differences in behaviour from the neoclassical capitalist firm thus had to look for other institutional peculiarities, such as the absence of some markets assumed by neoclassical theory. The earliest modelling of peasant semisubsistence farms was done by A.V. Chayanov in 1925 (Thorner, Kerblay, and Smith, ed. 1966), and expanded using modern mathematical techniques by Nakajima (1969). The key assumption was the absence of an off-farm labor market. As a result, the model indicated that an increase in family labor supply resulted in intensified production, driving down marginal productivity of labor while increasing output and income. A zero marginal productivity of labor could develop for on-farm activities.

The noticeable difference between the agricultural household model and the traditional models of households was the inclusion of the profit effect. Since the household model integrated the production and consumption of the farm household, the profit effect really made the result different from that of traditional household models. The difference appears not only in the elasticity of demand for agricultural commodities with respect to own-price, but also in the elasticity of demand for non-agricultural commodities and the elasticity of labor supply (SSS, 1986c).

The following sections review various prototypes of household model and their characteristics of utility function, demand function, and production function, estimation issues, such as separability and recursiveness, and previous empirical studies on agricultural household models.

2. Literature Review of Household Models

The Basic Model of Agricultural Household

The basic model of the agricultural household, as described below, was used in most previous empirical investigations. It was based on the choice-theoretic principle of maximizing the utility of the household subject to income and resource (land, capital and labor) constraints. Singh, Squire, and Strauss summarized it as follows:

Max $\qquad U = U (X_a, X_m, X_l)$

Subject to $P_m X_m = P_a (Q - X_a) - w (L - F)$ $\qquad$ (1)

$\qquad\qquad T = X_l + F$ $\qquad\qquad\qquad$ (2)

$\qquad\qquad Q = Q (L, A)$ $\qquad\qquad\qquad$ (3)

where U is the utility function, equations (1)-(3) are income, family time and production function constraints respectively; X_a is the agricultural staple, X_m is the market purchased good, X_l is leisure, P_m is the price of market purchased good, P_a is the price of the staple, Q is the household production function for the staple, w is the market wage, L is total labor input, F is the family labor input, T is total time available to family labor, and A is the fixed quantity of land of the household (*SSS* pp. 17).

The income constraint can be also written as:

$$P_m X_m + P_a X_a + w X_l = wT + \pi$$

where $\pi = P_aQ(L, A) - wL$ is the profit function. The left side of this equation is expenditure on three items, and right side is total income of the household. This formulation assumes the household's behaviour as a price-taker.

The income constraint is based on a "full income and full expenditure" concept, in which leisure is given an implicit value at the market wage and included as part of income and expenditure equations (Becker, 1965).

The household, therefore, can choose its consumption of a bundle of commodities, including leisure, and total labor input in production. To maximize utility, the first-order condition is derived. For the labor input:

$$P_a \, \partial Q / \partial L = w$$

The marginal product of labor equals the market wage rate. There is only one endogenous variable L, and the other three endogenous variables do not appear in this equation. Thus the demand for labor is independent of the commodities consumed by the household. The solution for the demand for labor is:

$$L^* = L^*(w, P_a, A).$$

If $Y^* = P_mX_m + P_aX_a + wX_l$ is defined as the full income of the household at the optimum for labor (production), the demand for the three commodities is:

$$X_i = X_i(P_m, P_a, w, Y^*).$$

Most farm households produce multiple products from both fixed and variable inputs, however. In this case, the income constraint becomes:

$$Y = \sum_{i=1}^{L} p_i X_i = p_t T + \sum_{j=1}^{M} q_j Q_j - \sum_{i=1}^{N} q_i V_i - p_t L + E$$

where X_is are consumed items (including X_L, leisure), p_i are consumer commodity prices, Q_i are products, V_i are variable inputs, q_j and q_i are product and input prices respectively, p_l is the wage rate, E is income exogenous to the farming operation, and other variables are as above. The utility function, defined over the multiple X_i and X_L, remains unchanged.

The production function may also be usefully generalized, using an implicit form to account for multiple products:

$$G(Q_1,...Q_m, V_1,...V_n, L, K_1,...K_o) = 0$$

where K_i's are fixed inputs. This function, which links inputs and outputs, is assumed to satisfy the usual properties of production functions -- quasi-convexity, increasing in outputs and decreasing in inputs (*SSS*, 1986). As a general specification, it allows separation of multiple outputs or joint production. In the usual case, provided the farmers are price-takers, introduction of multiple crops does not have an effect on the recursive property of the model (*SSS*, 1986).

For two crops, a food crop Q_c and a cash crop Q_a with market prices q_c and p_a respectively, the Lagrangian function, therefore, can be written as

$$\mathscr{L} = U(X_l, X_m, X_a) + \lambda[p_l T + (q_c Q_c + p_a Q_a - p_l L - q_v V)$$
$$+ E - p_l X_l - p_m X_m - p_a X_a] + \mu G(Q_c, Q_a, L, V, K).$$

where utility is maximized subject to the budget constraint and production function. In this case, the first-order conditions on production include the relationships:

$$\frac{1}{\lambda}\frac{\partial \mathcal{L}}{\partial Q_a} = p_a + \frac{\mu}{\lambda}G_a = 0$$

$$\frac{1}{\lambda}\frac{\partial \mathcal{L}}{\partial Q_c} = q_c + \frac{\mu}{\lambda}G_c = 0$$

The value of marginal product equals market price for both food and cash crops.

Extensions of the Models

Previous studies have extended the basic models to deal with special issues or special points of emphasis. Major extensions are to the utility function and constraints, including the income constraint and production function.

Utility Function. Normally, utility depends on consumption of a bundle of commodities, including leisure. However, if households are not demographically uniform, the form of utility function (and derivatives with respect to its arguments) can be expected to vary with the demographics. Adulavidhaya and others used two demographic factors, numbers of workers and numbers of dependents, in the utility function for the Thailand study (1984). The utility function becomes:

$$U = U (Z, A, C; a_1, a_2).$$

where a_1 is number of workers, and a_2 is number of dependents. When demand functions are derived by maximizing utility, these functions will also include demographic parameters.

If the household determines its production and consumption dynamically, the utility function has to reflect intertemporal choices. Roe and Graham-Tomasi (1986) used an additive, separable, time-invariant utility function, which was exponential in form, to estimate a risk impact on the household's production and consumption:

$$U (\{X_t, X_{1t}, b_t\} \, {}_{t=0}^{t=T})$$

where X_t and X_{1t} are consumption at periods t and t+1 respectively, and b_t is a financial asset held by the household.

Demand Function. The requirements of econometric estimation for reasonably simple equation forms to be used in estimating demand or expenditure equations lies behind most variation in assumptions about the utility function. Often it is easier to work from assumptions on the indirect utility function rather than assume an explicit equation form for the direct utility function.

For example, the Linear Expenditure System (LES) and Linear Logarithmic Expenditure System (LLES) are particularly easy to estimate because of the linearity property, but they can only be derived from indirect utility functions which are, unfortunately, restrictive in their properties. The LLES is derived from a translog indirect utility function homogeneous of degree minus one in prices, which implies unit expenditure elasticity with respect to full income for all commodities -- an unlikely assumption if many detailed food commodities are specified. The LES requires an additive utility function, which implies linear Engel curves and no Hicks-complementarity between commodities (again, problematic with particular foods).

The Quadratic Expenditure System (QES), though it requires non-linear econometric estimation procedures, can be derived from a class of indirect utility functions with reasonable properties -- specifically, quadratic Engel curves and inferior goods are allowed. That is, the budget proportion of food can decline with increased income, or absolute expenditure decline respectively. Its nonlinearity is offset by the limited number of parameters. Strauss (1986) used an indirect utility function in estimation of the determinants of food consumption and caloric availability in rural Sierra Leone, which uses full income -- profit plus exogenous income and total time -- in place of expenditure, with the form:

$$V = -\prod_{k=1}^{N} p_k^{\alpha_k} / (E + wT + \pi - \sum_{k=1}^{N} p_k c_k) + \prod_{k=1}^{N} p_k^{(\alpha_k - \delta_k)}$$

where c_k, α_k, and δ_k are parameters to be estimated from the data and

E = exogenous income,

p_k = prices of goods, k = 1,...,N - 1,

w = price of labor,

T = leisure time available to the household, and

π = short-run net income

= value of all outputs less the value of variable inputs

(excluding family labor)

and where $\sum_{k=1}^{N} \alpha_k = \sum_{k=1}^{N} \delta_k = 1$ (if the Nth "commodity" is leisure).

The term $E + wT + \pi$ is the households's full income[3].

Using Roy's identity (with full income replacing total expenditure), one can derive the QES expenditure equations:

$$p_iX_i = p_ic_i + \alpha_i \left(wT + \pi + E - \sum_{k=1}^{N} p_kc_k\right)$$
$$-(\alpha_i - \delta_i) \prod_{k=1}^{N} p_k^{(-\delta_i)} \left(wT + \pi + E - \sum_{k=1}^{N} p_kc_k\right)^2$$

where X_i = consumption of good i, i = 1, ..., N - 1

             X_N = household leisure.

This can be modified to accommodate household demographic variables.

     Production Function. The production function reflects the resource constraints on household production. Resources include the total inputs available in family production, including family endowment of labor and owned property (land, capital, etc.) as well as any purchased inputs. The form of the production function must provide for positive and decreasing marginal productivity of each factor in production, and output must approach a finite value as each individual factor input increases (Bridge, 1971). In simplified models, a constant technology status is always assumed (unless examining the effect of technology change).

---

[3] Note that the definition of T and π differs from that given in the preceding section, where T = total time endowment of family labor and the earnings of family labor at the market wage rate are deducted in arriving at farm profits (rather than net income). This is because π, as defined in this data set, does not deduct returns to family labor, and no information is available on its magnitude.

The most common form of production function used in analysis of agricultural production is the Cobb-Douglas (CD) production function, which assumes unit elasticity of substitution among inputs. The conventional form is:

$$Q = AL^{\alpha}K^{\beta}$$

where A is a technology coefficient, α and β are exponential coefficients for labor (L) and capital (K) respectively (additional terms might represent land or other factors of production). In logarithmic form it becomes:

$$\ln Q = a + \alpha \ln L + \beta \ln K \qquad \text{where } a = \ln(A).$$

Besides its log-linearity, the CD function provides a measure of relative efficiency (in the intercept term A); a measure of relative factor intensity (in the ratios between exponents); and a measure of returns to scale (in the sum of the exponential terms).

An alternative equation form, which allows the elasticity of substitution to differ from unity, is the constant elasticity of substitution (CES) function:

$$Q = \gamma[\delta K^{-\rho} + (1-\delta)L^{-\rho}]^{-v/\rho}$$

where γ is an efficiency parameter, δ is an intensity measure, v represents economies of scale, and the elasticity of substitution $\sigma = 1/(1+\rho)$. When $\sigma = 1$ ($\rho = 0$), the CES can be shown to reduce to a CD function; otherwise the nonlinearity of the CES presents estimation problems. When there are more than two factors of production, it is usually required that $\sum \delta_i = 1$. Unfortunately, the δ_i are not scale-independent of the factor inputs.

When there is more than one product Q_i, it is usual to assume completely separate production functions for each product (along with separation of factor inputs by product) or else to aggregate production using value added. The first approach is impossible if the data do not disaggregate input use (commonly the case for general household income surveys). The second approach <u>assumes</u> unconstrained profit maximization and complete markets -- assumptions which should be the subject of tests. Faced with this problem, Strauss (1981) assumes that outputs as a group are separable from inputs as a group, that is, the generalized production function described above can be re-written:

$$G(Q_1,...Q_m) = F(V_1,...V_n,L,K_1,...K_o)$$

where Q_j = output, for j = 1, ...m

          V_i = nonlabor variable inputs, for i = 1, ...n

          L = labor demand

          K_i's = fixed inputs.

If the individual commodity production functions are really entirely separate, this imposes some undesirable restrictions on behaviour (Lau, 1978), and can be justified mainly as an unavoidable approximation, and probably a better approximation if a single crop is dominant in production. On the other hand, if joint production -- e.g., intercropping or mixed multiple cropping systems -- is a major feature of farming practice (as it is in China), separability of outputs as a group from inputs as a group is a reasonable approximation.

Assuming this separability, it is still necessary to specify equation forms for both grouped outputs and grouped inputs. In order mainly to minimize the number of parameters, a Constant Elasticity of Transformation (CET) function for outputs (identical to the CES above, with outputs in place of inputs and $v=0$) and a CD function on the input side, normalized with $A=1$ can be used (Strauss, 1986). That is:

$$(\sum_{i=1}^{M} d_i Q_i^\rho)^{1/\rho} = \alpha L^{\beta_L} A^{\beta_A} K^{\beta_K}$$

Q_i = production of good i, $i = 1, ..., M$,

L = labor use (family plus hired),

A = total cultivated area,

K = capital flow, and all others are parameters.

The main advantage of this CET-CD multi-production functional form is its simplicity (minimum number of parameters). Also, the optimal product-mix ratios at given relative prices do not change (Powell and Gruen, 1968). Furthermore, the supply function derived by assuming profit maximization remains relatively simple -- among other things, with elasticities of output being the same for each output with respect to each input, fixed or variable.

If L is taken to be the variable input, with price w, and profits are maximized while other inputs are assumed fixed, the derived output-supply function (Strauss, 1986) is:

$$Q_i = \beta_L^{\beta_L/1-\beta_L} d_i^{-1/(\varphi-1)} p_i^{1/(\varphi-1)} \left(\sum_k d_k^{-1/(\varphi-1)} p_k^{\rho/(\varphi-1)}\right)^{(\varphi\beta_L-1)/\rho(1-\beta_L)}$$
$$(A^{\beta_A} K^{\beta_K})^{1/(1-\beta_L)} w^{[-\beta_L/(1-\beta_L)]}$$

where p_i are product prices and d_i, ρ and β_L are parameters.

Since in a competitive equilibrium (with complete markets, etc.), the marginal rate of transformation between outputs should equal the relative price ratios, it is worth noting that the CET requires that:

$$-\frac{\partial X_i}{\partial X_j} = \frac{\delta_j}{\delta_i}\left(\frac{X_j}{X_i}\right)^{1+\rho}$$ If ρ is close to zero, as noted above, the CES (and CET) reduces

to a log-linear form, which may be simpler to estimate.

Estimation Issues

Separability. Separability in models of producer-consumer units is usually defined as independence of production decisions from consumption decisions. Separability can usually be assumed when perfect markets in all inputs and outputs exist, with homogeneity of both products and inputs (including labor). Conversely, a single incomplete or imperfect market may lead to inseparability. The distinction between separable and non-separable household models is very important because improper estimation of the model would give misleading results.

Non-separability is found to be more common than separability in modelling certain circumstances, such as where the selling price differs from the purchase price for the same commodity, cases of incomplete markets and interlinked markets, and in cases of risk aversion or external incentives, and for household production activities (*SSS* Chapter 2). Non-separability has two impacts on the empirical model: (1) the comparative statics are complicated, and (2) statistical inconsistency can easily arise in demand and supply parameter estimation.

At one extreme, in subsistence agriculture, each household consumes its own produce, and the family labor supply and fixed endowments of other inputs provide the binding constraints on production. In this circumstance, production decisions are totally determined by consumption decisions, and complete inseparability exists. Nakajima (1969) elaborated the theoretical model, but did not pursue econometric estimation.

SSS (Chapter 2) summarizes three non-separability cases characteristic of semi-commercialized farm economies: (1) differing sales and purchase prices in the labor market, (2) incomplete and interlinked markets and risk, and (3) household production activities. In the first case, differences between sale and purchase prices can be caused by transportation cost, supervision cost, and heterogeneity of commodities. A differential preference between on-farm and off-farm labor may result from transportation of off-farm labor (Lopez, 1986). Family labor and hired labor are also not perfect substitutes due to supervision costs with hired labor. Heterogeneity of commodities can be interpreted as a differential between sale price and purchase price. Commodities include agricultural goods, non-agricultural goods, and labor. Non-separability is usually found in this case. For the same commodity, such as rice, quality differentials may result in different prices, e.g., for own-produced and market-purchased food. Under risk aversion, different attitudes toward own-produced and market-purchased food may be expressed as different demands for two kinds of foods. However, whether commodity heterogeneity results in non-separability depends on the household's choice of its consumption. If the household chooses a corner solution, in which it consumes all of its produce, then the virtual prices[4] of commodities may be higher or lower than the market prices, and non-separability occurs. If the household sells a part of its produce (interior solution), then the market price is the opportunity cost, and the production and consumption solutions are separable.

In the second case, interlinking of markets may result from incomplete markets, although empirical models have not generally reflected such interlinkages. For example, inability to access credit may cause share tenancy to develop, with tenants obtaining capital from landlords; or absence of a labor market may cause land lease or rental decisions to be affected by the stock of family laborers. Nonseparability in such cases relates only to the labor-leisure choice.

---

[4] Shadow prices, which are determined by the household's choices, and are a function of market prices, time endowment, fixed inputs, and either exogenous income or utility.

A major underlying source of incomplete and interlinked markets may be market or production risks. Sharecropping is one phenomenon attributable to risk in production, and has been analyzed using single period models (Bardhan and Srinivasan, 1971). Roe and Graham-Tomasi (RGT) developed a dynamic model to deal with risk in production. Their separability results have shown that if perfectly competitive markets exist for future contingencies and in other markets, and if products are assumed homogeneous, risk can be completely diversified away, leading to separability. Similarly, under risk neutrality, if competitive markets (input, output and financial) exist, production and consumption decisions are ensured separable. Under risk aversion, in RGT's model, to guarantee separability, the very restrictive assumptions are made that the utility function is additively separable over time, and each period's subutility is negative-exponential in form, consumption goods are homogeneous, and production risk is multiplicative and normally distributed. However, usually the existence of market and production risks will make it very difficult to maintain separability.

A third case, relevant mainly to studies of policies affecting family health and nutrition, relates to the interaction between family decisions on food intake, other health inputs, and health outputs, and decisions on labor input in farm production. However, if the household and hired labor are perfect substitutes, separability between production and other decisions still holds. For example, in a case study which dealt with the relationship among agricultural prices, food consumption, and the health and productivity of Indonesian farmers (Pitt and

Rosenzweig, 1986), the existence of a labor market was assumed. In this case, analysis of the model showed that, although the farmer's consumption and his labor productivity are interdependent, the choice of consumer goods and leisure is independent of farmer input (labor), and the farm's production and consumption decisions are separable. This was attributable to the perfect substitutability between farm labor and hired labor in the market at constant wage rates, so that the farm profit was independent of farmer's health status.

Recursive vs. Simultaneous Models. In a recursive model, there is a time sequence to decisions such that a clear path of causality can be discerned -- for example, decisions about production input are taken before the market prices of the product are exactly known. In a simultaneous model, decisions about all or most variables are taken at the same time and the directions of causality are not so clear -- e.g., decisions about production input both influence and are influenced by market prices. For econometric estimation of models, recursiveness is a convenient; conversely, when models are highly simultaneous, econometric estimation may prove difficult.

Separability is necessary for recursiveness to hold. Recursiveness property requires complete markets, that is all markets (input, output, and labor) exist, and the household is a price-taker. The commodities produced and consumed are homogenous (although this assumption can be relaxed). The households make their production and consumption decisions independently *and sequentially*, the production decisions first, followed by consumption decisions. Production and labor supply are not dependent on consumption preferences. Since the households are price-takers, market price variations determine extent of marketing and purchases of agricultural and non-agricultural goods. However, if households' production decision depends on both labor-supply (technology) and consumption-demand (preferences), separability doesn't exist, and recursiveness no longer holds. As long as one market does not exist, the property of complete recursiveness does not hold.

Even with complete markets, in the circumstance that the household consumes all of its produce (corner solution), there is no marketing activity, and the household's decisions concerning production and consumption are not separable, a *virtual price* exists, which is a function of preferences and technology. The process of decision-making is simultaneous. This is the case of subsistence agricultural households.

In the absence of perfect markets (e.g., homogeneous commodity, single price), the virtual prices in a model may be affected by market prices, without necessarily resulting in changes in decision variables. For example, if an on-farm wage (virtual price) differs from the market wage rate, family labor is an imperfect substitute for hired labor, and on-farm and off-farm employment are imperfect substitutes, then the virtual prices are affected by change in exogenous variables (*SSS*, 1986a).

In Lopez's (1986) study, for example, basic assumptions which result in a simultaneous model are imperfect substitution between family labor and hired labor in the utility and production functions, because the household's attitude toward on-farm work and off-farm work is different, which implies that the elasticity of labor supply to on-farm and off-farm uses differs. He found that quite different econometric estimates of these elasticities resulted from assumptions of recursiveness and simultaneity, respectively. However, if the variations in the exogenous variable (e.g., market wage) and the dependent variable of policy interest (e.g., elasticity of commercial sales with respect to market product prices) are not closely linked to the market that is cleared by the virtual price (e.g., on-farm labor market), the simultaneity would not be very important (SSS, 1986a). In such a case, estimation based on assumed recursiveness would probably not lead to seriously biased results.

Empirical Applications

A number of empirical studies estimated models of agricultural households to derive the optimum solutions for resource allocation. The first empirical studies included Yotopoulos, Lau, and Lin for Taiwan farms in 1976; Lau, Lin, and Yotopolous for Taiwanese farms in 1978; Koroda and Yotopoulos for Japanese farms in 1978 and 1980; Barnum and Squire for Malaysian farms in 1978 and 1979; and Adulavidhaya and others for Thai farms in 1979 and 1984. The common characteristics of these models were (1) econometric models, (2) separability assumption, (3) using cross-section data, but differing in the way the data was grouped (e.g., by household size or by region or by production and consumption), (4) using an equation system approach to estimation, such as a Log-linear Expenditure System, or Linear Expenditure System.

For policy consideration, the models provided insight to the policymakers on three aspects: (1) welfare of agricultural households, (2) spillover effect of agricultural policies on the entire rural economy, and (3) interrelationship between agricultural policy and other macroeconomic policies, e.g., trade policy, and fiscal policy. It seems to be advantageous for policymakers to consider the multiple effects of policies on both production and consumption relationships, and on distinct groups of people, such as net producers, net purchasers, and semicommercial households (*SSS*, 1986).

Whatever issues the models were targeted at, such as labor distribution, consumption and nutrition, or price policy, the object has always been to examine the effect of exogenous variables (e.g., market prices) on endogenous variables (normally output supply, marketed surplus, consumption of agricultural commodities and non-agricultural commodities, and labor supply). Elasticity analysis (derived from comparative statics, and estimated econometrically from household data) is commonly used to obtain empirical results. However, the response of endogenous to exogenous variables is not uniform in theory, rather varying depending on different assumptions and different situations in the theoretical models; and the comparative statics often leads to ambiguous signs. Not surprisingly, empirical results are also not uniform: for example, the response of the consumption of agricultural commodities to own-price was found to be positive in Taiwan, Malaysia and Rep. of Korea, while negative in Japan, Thailand and Sierra Leone (*SSS*, 1986).

Researchers studying the behaviour of farm households in developing countries acknowledge that food security is a major concern of farm households, especially low-income households; and that farmers are mostly risk averse, seeking food security before responding to marketing incentives (Hammer, 1986). This, however, is as far as the studies normally go in relating poverty, food security, and commercialization, although some models have tested the effect of market price variation on marketed surplus, income, and food consumption. Fafchamps (1992) comes closest to developing a household model which clarifies the relationship between expenditure on food consumption, income elasticity of food demand, and crop portfolio.

An alternative to clarifying these relationships through the mathematical solutions of a household model is to assume a standard or basic household model, but design the process of econometric estimation to explore these relationships. Strauss (1986) develops a standard separable household model for farmers in Sierra Leone. By assuming mathematical forms of consumption and supply functions flexible enough to reflect differences in price and income elasticities by income group, his econometric results can meaningfully be differentiated over income groups. Although his focus is not on the relationship between poverty, food security, and commercialization, Strauss' results can be used to draw conclusions about these relationships. This strategy will prove useful as we apply theoretical models in Chinese context following.

D. Summary

In this section, we have reviewed previous studies on (i) food security, poverty and commercialization, and (ii) agricultural household models. For the first, there have been a number of studies on the definition, causes, and measurement of poverty, food insecurity and commercialization. A common view was that poverty is the root cause of chronic food insecurity. Therefore, policies targeting food insecurity, such as food subsidies, income transfer programs, food prices stabilization, and public works (provision of employment opportunities), were always associated with poverty alleviation. However, building the poor's capacity to overcome poverty has more enduring results than poverty alleviation. Once poverty is overcome, food insecurity is likely to disappear. Thus an appropriate government strategy would include production-oriented policies, technological innovation, food aid for developmental purposes, and so on. These have been applied in many developing countries.

Urbanization, technological change, and non-agricultural sector development in rural areas are forces driving commercialization. Efforts at market integration, rural infrastructure improvement, and proper government policies, such as promotion of exports, are often considered necessary facilitators of commercialization. However, smallholders, who are risk-averse, will still allocate most of their land to food production due to "subsistence-first" (food security) concerns.

Many case studies, for example, by IFPRI and the World Bank, have looked at the impacts of commercialization on income, food consumption, and nutritional status by comparing ex ante and ex post situations and treating commercialization as an independent variable. However, the results of different studies have shown inconsistent impacts, positive or negative, and the subject remains controversial. The explanations given range from inconsistent research methodoogies to differences in the countries' political, economic and social conditionsm, and, as well, in government policies.

In this study, however, commercialization is viewed as a consequence of farmer decision making, and the relationship of the former to food insecurity and poverty is viewed as an association, rather than a cause-and-effect relation. Nevertheless, we will investigate whether associations commonly found in other developing countries, such as between food insecurity and poverty, would also apply in rural China. The issues of definition and measurement of poverty and food insecurity were reviewed here in order to provide a clear conceptual basis for distinguishing types of household. On commercialization, this study will focus on influences causing changes in marketing rates of households, i.e., promoting or hindering the commercialization process at the household level, especially for the poor.

Agricultural household models have been commonly employed in research on farmers' behavior in developing countries since 1980. Basically, such models describe the process of decision-making on production, consumption and labor supply of farm households. They are also used to examine the impacts of changes in prices, technology, and policy on households' wealth, consumption, and production in order to provide appropriate information to policymakers.

The fundamental difference between household models and traditional models of the firm is the inclusion in the former of the profit effect, which can influence the households' consumption and production responses (elasticities), since the household models integrate production and consumption together.

Previous empirical applications of household models have dealt with various problems, such as crop structure, determinants of food consumption, and risk in production. However, the empirical findings of previous studies were not uniform, due to differences in survey and econometric methodologies, economic circumstances (e.g., degree of commercialization), and possibly farmers' behavior.

This study intends to build an agricultural household model to deal with the relationship among poverty, food security and commercialization in rural China. The basic household model will be applied with modifications to constraints. The profit effect will be considered in elasticity analysis. Quadratic Expenditure System (QES) and Constant Elasticity Transformation and Cobb-Douglas (CET-CD) are the equation forms which will be used to estimate consumption and production functions econometrically.

III. POVERTY, FOOD SECURITY AND COMMERCIALIZATION: THE CHINESE CONTEXT

A. Pre-Reform Period (1949-1979)

Food security was one of the serious issues facing the Chinese government after the founding of the People's Republic of China in 1949. Land reform, which took place over several years, redistributed land among individual households based largely on the number of family members (Perkins, 1966; Walker, 1965). The relative equalization of resources among farmers for the first time led to a general sense of household food security.

In the urban areas, facing inflationary pressures and instability in the grain market, the government made great efforts to stabilize the market. In 1953, the policy of "Unified Procurement and Sales" (tonggou tongxiao UP&S) was introduced, as both a means of stabilization and a mechanism for resource transfer to the industrial sector. Under this policy, the government monopolized the grain market through procurement quotas and rationed distribution of grain and other agricultural products. The policy was promoted as a contribution to social welfare, especially to provide food security for low-wage urban residents, and price stability and marketing security for farmers. As it developed over time, however, its main objective was providing low-cost raw materials and wage goods for the industrial sector and thereby facilitating a high rate of capital accumulation rather than transfer of surpluses from agriculture through low procurement prices (Song, 1987).

Planning crop planting area was an important aspect of the UP&S system. The administrative structure established under the cooperatives (1953-1958) and communes (1958-1983) served to facilitate the implementation of planned production and sales (Song, 1987).

The rationing system -- including procurement quotas based on consideration of local food, feed, and seed requirements -- provided a general food security for the entire population. Security was defined in terms of quantities of grain and other basic foodstuffs, however, not in nutritional status or quality.

1. Planning System

For such a large country with millions of firms and households, especially facing an economy devastated from the anti-Japanese war and civil war, the Chinese government had to choose a system for direction of its economic activities. The system of central planning, as operating in the Soviet Union, was regarded as the best means of managing a "socialist" economy. In order to convey the government's messages to the entire society and get feedback information from the bottom as soon as possible, every economic activity -- production, marketing, and distribution -- had to be controlled through planning.

A Five-Year Plan served to guide the general course of economic development, by setting the goals, general production targets for each sector of national economy, rate of accumulation, price levels, and income level. The state also employed annual production plans, using a "material-balance planning" framework, based on the Five-Year Plan. "Marketing", in such a system, becames a matter of distribution of resources and products among sectors. The State Planning Commission assigned a given amount of products (not properly called commodities) to enterprise users at planning prices, termed allocation prices. The output of enterprises was similarly assigned to other sectors as inputs, and to the commercial organs as final products to consumers. All these products were valued at planning prices, which were not necessarily related to either scarcity or production cost.

The state-owned enterprises submitted enterprise taxes to the state. The remaining revenues were used for re-investment and distribution to employees at the state-unified wage scales. The general wage rates were determined by the state as scales depending on the education level, types of work, and length of work experience.

Consumer goods were wholesaled by the factories to the state-owned and collective-owned commercial companies at state-regulated prices. Retail trade was largely monopolized by state and collective stores, and retail prices were also determined by the state.

2. Planning System in Rural Areas

Grain Production Planning

The management of grain production experienced a transition from individual household producer to collective, cooperative and commune; and from unplanned to planned during this period. As the government increasingly suppressed private trade and took control of the distribution system, it also took upon itself responsibility for providing food security. However, the administrative control system for distribution was only concerned with guaranteeing the food requirements of urban areas. Whether, because it was incapable of managing distribution in the rural areas, or because this would have conflicted with extractive goals, a self-sufficiency orientation in basic food supply became a necessity for the rural areas. This was enshrined in Mao's general slogan to "take grain as key link", which was the foundation of agricultural policy for about two decades (from 1958).

The administrative mechanism of grain production planning centred on the Ministry of Agriculture, which imposed output and sown area targets for major grains (rice, wheat, and corn). These annual targets were then distributed among provinces based on cultivated area and average yield; and similarly subdivided among counties by the province, and among communes by the county; and finally among brigades and teams by the commune (Crook, 1991; Groen and Kilpatrick, 1978).

The farmers' "private plot" (Zi-liu di), limited to 5% of the total land the team owned was the only exception to this vertically-integrated planning system. This plot was an important supplementary source of food and income, commonly used to grow vegetables for self-consumption or cash sale or feed for animals. At times it was also used as a supplementary source of staple food. (Walker, 1984).

Marketing System in Agricultural Sector

In the agricultural sector, free trade in agricultural products prevailed until 1953, when the government, faced with soaring market prices of grain, decided to implement UP&S in order to stabilize the grain market and guarantee urban residents' grain supply, especially to government employees who were paid low wages. This system was the core of the agricultural planning system, although it did not initially extend to the entire agricultural products market.

Following the initiation of UP&S, collectivization in the rural areas began in earnest in 1955. By 1958, the institutional reform in rural areas was completed by organizing the farmers within the highest administrative level -- the people's commune. The institutional organization provided insurance that government's rural policies would be implemented without direct conflict between the state and individual farmers.

Under the UP&S policy, procurement quotas applied to grains, cotton, and edible oil, which were classified as first-class commodities which could only be sold to the state (tong-gou). Livestock products and other major cash crops, such as tobacco, jute, sugarcane and sugarbeet, fruit and vegetables, were referred to as second-class commodities, sold to the state through contracts, which assigned the quantity the state wanted to purchase to the communes (pai-gou). These contracts were not voluntary, but compulsory obligations. Other commodities, which were not so significant to economic life or livelihoods, were not highly restricted, and either sold in the market or to the state. By 1978, the state procurement was 92% of total value of marketed agricultural products through quota and contracts (RGCCRA, 1989).

The quota was supposed to be fulfilled if grain production reached levels associated with normal weather; and 40% of any production exceeding targets was also supposed to be sold to the state.

Quotas were derived from the average output of grain in a normal year, subtracting estimated requirements for seed, human consumption (at standards varying by region), and feed (only for the collective animal herd, not for household backyard animal raising). The quota levels (after 1965) were supposed to be unchanging for three years (after 1971, for five years), but in practice were unchanged over much longer periods. In normal years, farmers were obligated to fulfil the quota, but in years of drought, flood, or severe insect damage, the quota could be reduced or waived depended on the degree of disaster (Wu, 1989). The level of the quota in general was too high to leave much surplus for marketing (indeed, seed and feed were retained by the production team, leaving only basic human consumption requirements for the households). As with crop area and production targets, procurement quotas were assigned from the top down through various levels of government to each production team. Besides quota procurement, the land tax was another stable and predictable source of grain procurement. The tax was paid in kind (in grain, for grain-producing areas), at rates based on average land productivity and which were, in practice, hardly ever adjusted. Crop purchases were the less predictable source of procurement (Perkins, 1966).

Quota prices were fixed with modest regional differentials, and only changed when there was a compelling need to improve farming incentives or meet costs of increased input use. Beginning in 1965, a 15% price differential was offered for sales above the quota, increased to 30% after 1971. Although in the early 1950s official procurement prices had been initially based on a "normal" market price level, subsequent adjustments took as reference production costs (including labor at a low accounting wage rate, but excluding any margin for land "rent"), and over time the margin between revenue and cost contracted to the point that little "profit" was left for either the collective or individual farmers.

The sale of grains was also monopolized by the government. Private grain traders were not allowed to operate, except as agents of the state grain companies (Gao, 1987). In the urban areas, the state-owned grain shop was the only legal place for the urban residents to purchase their rationed grain. Over three decades almost no adjustments were made to ration prices, even when quota procurement prices were increased. During this time the margin to cover transport, processing, and distribution costs erodes to the point that ration prices were lower than quota procurement prices, implying a substantial subsidy to urban residents.

In the rural areas, the state resold grain to four groups of people: (1) rationing for the grain-short households in grain growing areas; (2) farmers in cash-crop growing areas; (3) areas subject to natural disasters; and (4) the rural, non-agricultural population (of wage-workers). However, the rural resale price was higher than the urban ration price (Wu, 1989), generally covering distribution costs.

In 1984, resales of foodgrains were about 30% of the total procurement, while in 1985, they increased to 50% of the total procurement.

Food deficit households -- often among the poorest families -- were not necessarily in a position to purchase grain. In general, however, they were distributed the grain anyway, accumulating (paper) debts to the production team (as also the poorest production teams accumulated debts to the commune). (The official poverty group -- the "five-guarantee households" -- received free food distribution.)

Rural resales were not a central responsibility. The central government was primarily concerned with supplying the three provincial-level municipalities (Beijing, Tianjin, and Shanghai), two industrial provinces (Liaoning, a coal and steel production base, and Shanxi, a coal production base), and the military. Grain-surplus provinces faced a quota obligation to provide grain transfers for the above areas, at a unified price. Direct inter-provincial trade in grain was prohibited, i.e., two provinces could not negotiate grain trade themselves without central government intervention. Under this unified-price transfer system, the grain-surplus provinces, like Heilongjiang and Jilin, could not fully exploit their comparative advantage.

Rural resales were the responsibility of the provinces, although their grain requirements for such purposes could be treated as a subtraction when negotiating provincial obligations to supply grain to the central government. The provincial government was also expected to ensure its urban residents' rations from its own procurement from surplus rural areas. Thus the provinces also were pressured into pursuing a food self-sufficiency policy (Walker, 1984).

Related to this procurement policy, other restrictions on marketing of agricultural products, such as closure of markets, prohibition of regional trade or long-distance private trade, were all imposed. In addition, policies on the production side were made to assist procurement policies: (1) labor mobility was restricted in order to reduce labor cost; (2) land transfer (trade) was prohibited in order to control the effect of rent on the prices of agricultural products; and (3) production scale and diversification were restricted (Gao, 1987).

The UP&S also controlled the agricultural inputs market. The farmers (in fact, the communes) were not able to directly purchase manufactured inputs. Chemical fertilizer and pesticides were distributed to the commune at list prices under the various plans. In addition, inputs were exchanged for the procurement of cash crops and livestock products.

The UP&S policy made its positive contributions during the period of recovery from the war. These were (i) stabilizing retail prices of foodgrains and major agricultural products in urban areas (through low-priced procurement from farmers and stable retail prices to urban residents), the costs of industries using agricultural products as raw materials, and thereby, the general price level; (ii) accumulating a great volume of capital for industrialization; (iii) stabilizing supply to urban residents and industry; and (iv) imposing income equality (Gao, 1987).

However, the UP&S policy had the serious weakness that its low-priced procurement in fact was equivalent to imposing a heavy tax in kind. The procurement system meant imposing a system of distribution of benefits among the farmers, the state, and the urban consumers. The state reached its goal mainly through sacrifice of the farmers' benefit. This procurement system discouraged farmers from expanding and diversifying production (Gao, 1987).

Food Consumption

Until 1981, the Chinese government did not publicly (or officially) release statistical data on consumption. It was therefore impossible for western researchers to do reliable or detailed analysis. Nevertheless, a number of studies (e.g., by Liu and Yeh, Wiens, Walker, Piazza, and Lardy) have estimated the food consumption of the Chinese people, basing their estimates mainly on grain production statistics, sometimes supplemented with fragmentary consumption figures cited in Chinese newspapers or journals.[5] A series giving average national food consumption in urban and rural areas during 1952-83 was first published by SSB in 1984 (Figure 1). These figures are based on production-distribution balance sheets estimated by the Foodgrains Bureau of the Ministry of Commerce. They indicate the size of year-to-year fluctuations, which left precariously low consumption levels in the rural areas in the early 1960s and also in 1972. Despite the heavier energy requirement of rural labor, the series also show that urban residents were relatively favored during most of this period -- a measure of the success of the procurement system.

---

[5] "Grain", in Chinese statistical terminology, is inclusive of tubers (primarily sweet potatoes), counted as grain-equivalents at 4:1 (1950s-1964) or 5:1 (from 1964).

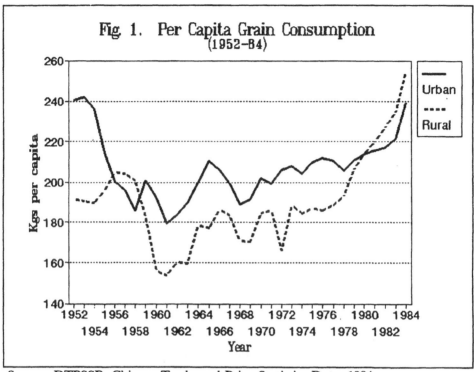

Fig. 1. Per Capita Grain Consumption
(1952–84)

Source: DTPSSB: Chinese Trade and Price Statistics Data, 1984

Rural food consumption data were estimated from sample surveys by the State Statistical Bureau beginning in 1954. Sample sizes were relatively small in early years (e.g., 16,000 households in 1954, but only about 6,000 households as late as 1978), but increased sharply during the 1980s, when the sample size approached 66,000. The consumption estimates based on the sample surveys are significantly higher than those constructed from consumption balance sheets[6]. The inconsistencies are probably mainly due to sample error and bias, as the estimates

---

[6] The two are not easily compared, since the survey data are given in terms of unmilled grain, whereas the balance sheets were constructed on the basis of "trade grain", which includes rice and millet on a milled basis.

tend to converge in the mid-1980s. It is likely, therefore, that the surveys overstate average consumption in the years 1978-82 and correspondingly understate later growth relative to these years.

The rural grain consumption during the 1950-1979 period was characterized by insufficient quantity and low quality, combined with regional disparities. Following the Great Leap (1958), for two decades, per capita grain consumption in the rural areas did not regain the levels reached in the early 1950s (Figure 1). Quantity retained in the rural areas for consumption was variable, inasmuch as it was the residual after procurement quotas (relatively stable) were fulfilled. Consumption quality reflected, first, the government's practice of procuring only rice and wheat, leaving the "coarse grains" (corn, millet, sorghum, and tubers) for self-consumption. It was also the outcome of a conflict of interest between the farmers (or production teams) and the government procurement agencies, which paid low prices and offered inadequate quality differentials: farmers preferred to sell their worst quality grain (in terms of variety, moisture content, and impurities) and government tried to obtain the best quality.

"Adequate quantity" of food, of course, must be evaluated in terms of human nutritional intake. Piazza (1986) has estimated the nutrient (energy, protein, and fat) availability (1950-82) of the Chinese people based on estimated national food balance sheets, covering most major food groups (grains including soybean and tubers, peanuts, vegetable oil, sugar, fruit, red meat, and fish). The estimates depend critically on his ability to identify the proportions of non-human food end uses (seed, feed, manufacturing, and losses during processing, transport, and storage; changes in stock are ignored), but for many of these uses, fragmentary or no data are available and assumptions must be made. Piazza also estimates per capita energy requirements based on FAO/WHO (1973) standards. These requirements were estimated to increase at a rate of about 0.3% per annum because of a changing population age distribution and average body weight for age. For protein, minimum standards are ill-defined, because the digestibility, which varies by source, is a key variable; moreover, if energy intake is inadequate, protein is converted to energy rather than being utilized for growth or repair.

Given the long term series of rural consumption data now available, it is possible to develop nutrient intake estimates which avoid the uncertain parameters required to construct food balance sheets (Figure 2). Complete series for 1952-83 cover per capita consumption of grain, pork, eggs, edible oil, and sugar (SSB, 1984). Other food groups accounting for about 10% of energy and 12% of protein (vegetables, beef and mutton, fish and shrimp) are only available for selected years (1954, 1956-57, 1965, 1978-84) (Taylor and Hardee, 1985) from the rural sample surveys (which, as noted above, are probably biased upwards for early years); the proportions of energy and protein they accounted for were extrapolated to the missing years and used to estimate total nutrient.

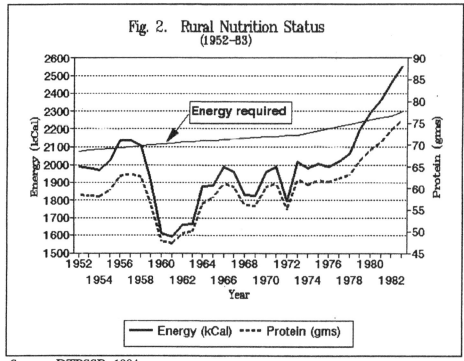

Fig. 2. Rural Nutrition Status
(1952–83)

Source: DTPSSB, 1984

Comparing the energy intake to energy requirements, it seems that, after reaching an adequate level in 1956-58, rural per capita energy intake fell drastically below requirements following the Great Leap, which resulted in an increased death rate reflecting 7-10 million deaths attributable to starvation. Rural energy intake only regained sufficiency in 1979, after the initiation of rural reforms. Protein intake consistently exceeded Piazza's estimate of "safe levels". However, because of the energy shortage, some of the "surplus" protein was converted to energy. Moreover, most of the protein came from plant rather than animal sources (about 90% in 1978), and therefore had a lower utilization rate. It is clear enough that rural Chinese <u>on</u>

average suffered chronic food insecurity during the era of collective agriculture and unified food procurement and sales.

However, regional disparity is the major remaining issue of food distribution in China, especially in the rural areas. Regional disparity of consumption was associated with production disparity, basically due to varying natural endowments, climate, and population density. For example, average per capita grain production in 1952-57 ranged from 223 kg. in Hebei to 596 kg. in Heilongjiang. Subtracting from production estimates of seed and feed requirements, four provinces (Henan, Hebei, Shanxi, and Guizhou) at that time produced too little to provide their populations with adequate levels of grain consumption (grain consumption availability was less than 1,800 KCal per capita) (Walker, 1984).

Estimates of the proportion of the rural population which suffered from chronic food insecurity have been compiled at various times, but differ considerably due to varying estimation methods and definitions of food deficit consumption levels. One set of estimates indicated that in 1952-57 about 18% of the rural population permanently produced insufficient grain, of which group about 36% were specialized cash crop producers, 12% were engaged in non-farm occupations, and the remainder were simply poor or living in low yielding areas (cited in Walker, 1984) Walker's estimates, based on provincial production figures, suggest that areas containing as much as 30% of the rural population were "food deficit", defined as a per capita production level of 275 kg unprocessed grain (yielding consumption of 1,700-1,900 KCal per capita, after deduction for seed and feed uses) (Walker, 1984).

Initially, procurement and resale policy was intended to partially -- but never completely -- even out such disparities among regions and even households. However, from the closure of the grain market in 1957, and the assumption of sole grain distribution responsibility by the state, the volume of grain re-distributed in rural areas apparently began to decline. A provincial "self-sufficiency" policy promoted after 1966 accentuated this trend. What remained of interregional redistribution of grain was the transfer of surplus grain from a few provinces (e.g., Heilongjiang, Jilin, Hubei, Jiangxi) to supply the three municipalities and two industrially-developed provinces (with more wage-workers than other provinces). The distribution of grain to chronically grain-deficit provinces, always dependent on availability of supplies, virtually ceased from the beginning of the Cultural Revolution (1966). Although there are no statistical data to document this, the implication is that the self-sufficiency oriented government policy increased regional disparities in consumption (Lardy. 1982).

B. The Reform Period of 1979-1990

For three decades, the Chinese government tried to provide food security for the entire population and realize income equalization. However, all this was executed by a sacrifice of the farmers' benefit. Poverty was one of the major consequences of the policy's implementation. The reform practices implemented after 1978 abandoned the goal of income equalization in the hope of lifting large numbers of farmers out of poverty.

1. Institutional Reform

This was aimed at encouraging households, rather than the collective, to resume direct responsibility for crop production and supply a fixed, contracted amount of their produce to the collective (bao chan dao hu), the remainder being marketable to the state at negotiated prices or (with the notable exception of grain) on the free market. Introduced initially in one-third of the counties judged "poverty areas," this "production responsibility system" (sheng chan ze ren zhi, PRS) rapidly spread to other areas, entirely replacing the collective system by 1983. Every household was assigned plots of land from the collective (in addition to their original "private plot") for a tenure which in due course was fixed at 15 years. Farmers were increasingly allowed to decide which crops to grow, how much inputs to use, and how much output to retain or market -- though not without restrictions or administrative pressures (RGCRDI, 1984).

The initial distribution of land followed a mix of egalitarian and efficiency principles (considering both household size and labor power), and consequently led to land fragmentation and small-scale farming with a self-sufficiency orientation. Moreover, land remained collective property and its sale or subleasing by recipient households was technically illegal. There were also collective enterprises with assets which could not easily be divided among households without undermining or destroying productivity. Thus from the beginning some households or groups became specialized in production by contracting responsibility to manage collective assets --

commonly in livestock raising, processing, orchards, and agro-services such as transport and construction.

However, the government recognized potential gains from land consolidation and specialization along lines of comparative advantage, including a higher proportion of marketed surplus (promoting commercialization), economies of scale in production, and increased receptiveness to mechanization. Entire areas were encouraged or allowed to increase their degree of specialization in cash crops, resuming patterns of production based on longstanding comparative advantage. With attractive opportunities in non-farm occupations attracting some households away from agricultural production, means were even found to facilitate land transfer and farm consolidation. It was far easier for the state procurement system to manage contractual relationships with a lesser number of highly commercialized agricultural producers, hence by the mid-1980s procurement work concentrated on so-called "commercial production bases," i.e., areas where high productivity, low man-land ratios, or a high degree of specialization led to large marketable surpluses. Positive publicity and administrative support were even given to consolidation of farms into the hands of "specialized grain households" -- producers who felt they could profitably manage the farmland (and meet the sales responsibilities) of other households.

Dramatic changes took place in the rural areas in the following few years. Besides continued bumper harvest of grain (the output reached a historical peak in 1984) -- the food security problem was generally solved -- the rural economic structure was also changed. Rural industry and other non-farming activities were

growing very fast. Rural labor engaged in non-farming occupations rose from 4%
of the total in 1978 to 11% in 1984 and 21% in 1990. Rural per capita net income
increased from 134 yuan in 1978 to 355 yuan in 1984 and 630 yuan in 1990 (in
current prices; in constant 1978 prices, the 1984 and 1990 incomes were 213 and 299
yuan respectively) (DASSSB, 1985-1991). Labor migration occurred, not only from
farming to non-farming occupations, but also from rural to urban areas, as well as
among regions. However, this did not occur uniformly, and regional disparity still
exists. The trend to commercialization did not develop evenly, and new issues of
poverty were brought out in the middle of the 1980s.

2. Procurement and Marketing System Reform

At the national level, the long-term problems of grain shortage and food
deficiency in the rural areas were solved early in the 1980s. Indeed, in 1984-1985
production so exceeded consumption requirements that state procurement could not
cope: available storage facilities were overflowing, and considerable grain had to be
stored in mat sheds, in the open, or at the household level. Free market grain prices
for once fell below the price at which the state was supposed to serve as "buyer of
last resort" (Gao, 1989a).

Facing the problems of under-capacity of storage and stocks well in excess
of requirements, and the opportunity presented by the collapse of free market prices,
the Chinese government decided to introduce a one-price contract procurement to
replace the multi-priced administrative pricing system. The contract price was equal

to 30% of previous quota price plus 70% of the previous above-quota price (in effect, 135% of the previous quota price, or 90% of the previous above-quota price). It was intended that contract procurement would be at a level of 50% of the previous year's procurement, so as to reduce the financial burden of procurement and storage; and procurement efforts would concentrate on commercial grain bases, leaving other areas free to sell on the free market or to government (at the government's discretion) at "negotiated prices"[7] (Crook, 1988; Gao, 1989a).

This reform did not succeed for a variety of reasons. Unlike previous administrative price reforms, the net impact on farm incentives to grow grain was negative: although the average procurement price was about the same as before, the marginal price to farmers who were able to sell more than the quota was reduced. Moreover, the government was no longer obligated to buy everything that farmers were willing to sell (previously farmers could obtain at least the above-quota price from government for sales exceeding the quota). In addition, reductions in input subsidies (1984) caused a price increase for manufactured inputs (fertilizer, fuel, electricity, etc.) of 16% in 1985 (Gao, 1987). Moreover, free market prices of grain sales had declined due to market abundance. The government also dropped administrative pricing of livestock procurement in 1985, causing increased demand for feedgrains in 1986 and a resumed growth of free market grain prices. Consequently the government could no longer count on voluntary contracts supplying

---

[7] "Negotiated prices" are prices near to market levels, though administratively set rather than being truly negotiated.

procurement, and was forced to make the contracts compulsory -- i.e., to restore the quota system.

Although the existence of parallel state and free market for agricultural products was legitimized by the reforms and the role of the free market has been allowed to gradually expand, the government has managed to retain control of the grain trade through its procurement of the majority of the marketable surplus to provide for the needs of urban and rural wage workers and cash crop producers, accumulation of reserves and industrial uses. Only a small residual is traded on the free market. In most countries, with such a parallel market structure, farmers are in a position to compare prices in the administered and free markets and make production and marketing decisions accordingly. In view of the high volume of compulsory sales to government in the early 1980s and the continuing state resale of grain to households specializing in cash crops, livestock raising, etc., it could be questioned whether the free market in China had much direct influence on farmer production and marketing decisions for grains (Gao, 1989a). However, negotiated prices, even though administratively determined, did move in parallel with market prices, and voluntary sales to government at negotiated prices were substantial in some years previous to 1985.

Beginning from 1985, there was no doubt that the importance of voluntary sales at negotiated and market prices grew sharply. According to national trade statistics, compulsory sales to the state, about 79% of total grain marketing in 1985, declined to about 49% by 1987 (DASSSB, 1987-1990). A 1989 survey of 93 counties confirms that (compulsory) contract procurement was only 45.1% of the total traded grain (Gao, 1990). This trend arose partly because, from 1985, the government distribution system stopped supplying grain to the industrial sector (breweries, bakeries, and pharmaceutical), catering service for trains, planes, and ships, and restaurants and hotels, forcing these sectors to shift to market purchase. However, grain transactions remained overwhelmingly between farmer and government: the major change was a reduction in compulsory contract procurement relative to voluntary negotiated-price procurement. Compulsory procurement was first reduced in 1985 in reaction to surpluses and excess stocks following the bumper harvest of 1984. Poor harvests in 1985-87 forced the government to turn increasingly to negotiated-price procurement to meet total procurement targets (Gao, 1989a).

Central government restrictions on inter-provincial grain trade were lifted in 1982. This trade was conducted on a negotiated price basis between surplus and deficit provinces (Wu, 1989). From 1983, private traders were allowed by central policy to engage in transport and sale of grain across provincial lines. However, provincial governments tended to restrict or prevent such trade whenever the volume reached levels threatening fulfilment of local procurement requirements -- for example, when Guangdong Province, a rapidly industrializing food deficit area, encouraged inflows of grain from neighboring Hunan, the latter promptly clamped down on grain exports.

On the retail side, the urban ration system was maintained, with no adjustment of prices until May 1991 (although, along side ration grain, high-quality grain was sold in urban areas without rationing and at negotiated prices beginning in 1985). At that time the government raised the urban retail price of grains by 54% (increased average 0.2 yuan), replacing it with a (partial) cash subsidy to retail price (the government subsidized 0.6 yuan for each kilogram of grain). This adjustment was expected to reduce government grain subsidies by about one-third (Xinhua Dispatches, 1991).

The market reforms did not bring complete liberalization of markets. The input markets were only partially freed: major inputs, such as agricultural machinery and fertilizer, were still subject to planning, but under the reforms, a portion were sold outside the plan at so-called negotiated prices (in effect, market prices). Land and labor markets were still highly restricted. The farmers were to have usufruct rights to land under a 15-year lease with the government, but did not have legal rights to trade it freely. In parallel with growth of non-farming activities, a labor market grew up in which laborers could be freely hired in or out, at negotiated wage rates. The formal credit market also expanded its volume of lending, though mainly for production purposes rather than non-production activities (Feder et al., 1991). No insurance market has yet emerged or been created to protect against price or production risk in farming, however.

Private trading companies for manufactured inputs and outputs have emerged as the free markets grew in scope. Private tradesmen were characterized by flexibility. They consisted of individuals, groups or cooperatives, with varying trading volume, some local and others interregional in activities. In 1978 there were about 136,000 full-time private traders, while in 1988 there were 11.06 million (SSB, 1990).

3. Food Consumption

The economic reform brought positive and negative consequences. One of the negative consequences for farmers was the loss of benefits ("socialist" privileges) from the collective, such as medical care. Such policies as allocation of land partly based on household labor supply, increased specialization, growth of non-farm activities of rural labor, and land consolidation all implied an abandonment of egalitarian principles of food distribution. The guarantee of food security became a household responsibility, and the food security issue increasingly became an inter-household problem, as well as continuing to be an inter-regional problem. For households with both abundant labor power and significant off-farm opportunities, food security could now be purchased with the cash income gains from commercial production or off-farm activities. However, poor households -- usually lacking labor resources, farming in low-yield areas, or with few cash income earning opportunities -- now faced a new security problem.

As a result of the increased farm income levels, farmers' overall consumption levels have improved significantly. In this process, caloric value of food consumption has increased, but the diversification of the diet has been most remarkable. Rural direct per capita grain consumption rose only 5.6% (248 kg. to 262 kg., in terms of unprocessed grain) from 1978 to 1990, according to farm household surveys; but "fine grain" (rice and wheat) consumption rose 75.5% (122.5

kg. to 21 kg.) during the same period. Indirect consumption of grain -- that is, consumption of livestock products fed on grain and byproducts -- also grew rapidly: in 1978 meat (red and white) consumption was 6 kg per capita per year, and rose to 12 kg in 1985, and 13 kg in 1990.

On average, the energy intake of the rural population rose from around 2,190 KCal per capita in 1978 to 2,347 KCal in 1985 (not adult equivalent), well above the estimated nutritional requirement (based on Piazza's estimation of 2270 KCal per capita). Protein intake rose from 55 g to 57 g in the same time period, with increasing meat consumption replacing reduced protein from grain.

However, not all areas shared equally in these gains. For example, ten provinces still were deficient in energy intake by the end of the 1980s (Figure 3), though almost all provinces met minimum protein requirements (Figure 4). During the 1980s, concern arose that some segments of the population, indeed, some areas of the country were not sharing in the general rural progress. This concern led to official identification of the so-called "poor areas", for purposes of monitoring their progress and implementing compensatory programs.

Aside from regional disparities, seasonal food shortage (a deficit of about one quarter's requirements) in well-developed and moderately-developed areas (east coast and central provinces) exists in low-income households (about 15-20% of the total). The major cause is high dependency relative to numbers of active, healthy laborers, especially male laborers. Such households usually get assistance from village government or relatives during deficit seasons.

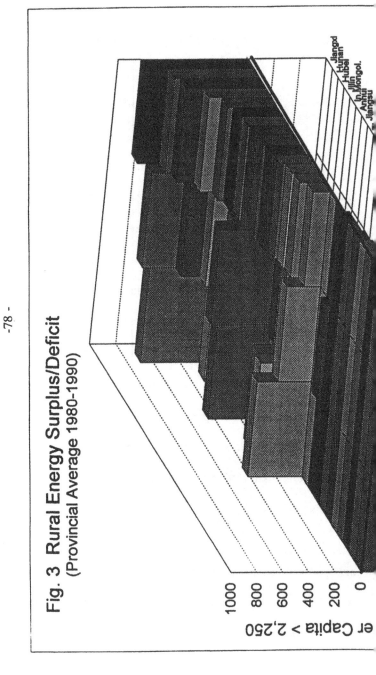

Fig. 3 Rural Energy Surplus/Deficit
(Provincial Average 1980-1990)

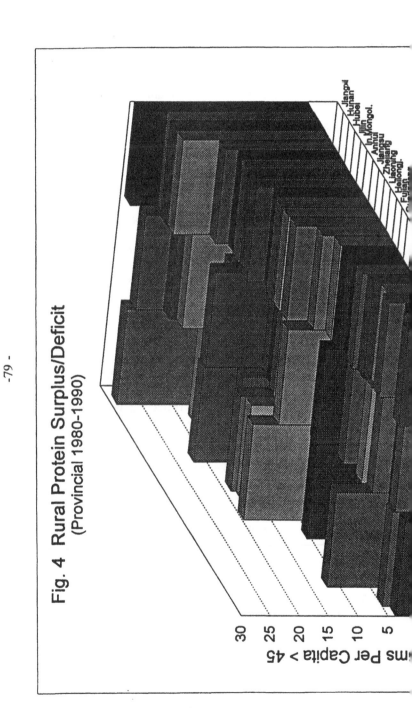

Fig. 4 Rural Protein Surplus/Deficit
(Provincial 1980–1990)

4. The Trend of Commercialization

The trend to commercialization did not develop evenly throughout the country: in well-developed areas with favorable natural endowment (geographic location, soil, climate, water sources, and so on), such as the coastal areas and suburbs of large cities, commercialization was swift, as in Beijing, where the commercialization rate of agricultural products grew from 34% in 1983 to 75% in 1988 (measured in constant prices). In underdeveloped areas, such as mountainous and minority areas, commercialization also grew, but less rapidly. For example, in Gansu, China's poorest province, it was 31% in 1983 and had only reached 42% in 1988 (CAYEC, 1990). These different trends were caused by various factors. Besides unfavorable natural environment, underdeveloped areas suffered from poorly developed marketing systems, reflecting lack of marketable surplus, inadequate infrastructure (transportation, communication) and government's restrictive interventions in the marketing system.

A general examination of provincial statistics on the extent of agricultural commercialization during 1983-88 suggests some of the issues which need further study.[8] These data show that agricultural commercialization (sales divided by total

---

[8] The data used here compare sales of agricultural products with gross agricultural income, where the latter includes self-consumption. Sales were valued at actual procurement or market prices (rising rapidly during the period), self-consumption at quota procurement prices (relatively stable). To distinguish "real" increase in commercialization from the differential impact of price escalation, it was necessary to deflate sales and self-consumption using separate price indices, to measure each in constant (1983) prices. Moreover, the statistical definition of

agricultural product) increased in every area during the 1980s, from an average of 34% in 1983 to 51% in 1988. There were, however, considerable regional differences in commercial rates which, in 1983, ranged from 17% to 49% in different provinces; and in 1988 ranged from 41% to 75%.

Figure 5 shows the regional differences in commercial rates in 1986, by which time most marketing restrictions had been removed. The regional patterns do not really fit the most common generalizations: (a) not all coastal areas had highly commercialized agriculture (see Fujian, Zhejiang, and Shanghai for example); (b) not all poor areas were very subsistence-oriented (e.g., Yunnan, Ningxia, Anhui, Shaanxi, and Shanxi all had commercial rates over 35%).

The (regression-estimated) trend rates of growth in commercialization over the 1983-88 period in each province show a bimodal distribution -- one large group of provinces commercialized rather slowly (+ 5-10% p.a.), another equally large group extremely rapidly (+ 15-20% p.a.). Multiple regression indicates that provinces which initially were less commercial and/or had high initial per capita incomes tended to commercialize most rapidly during this period. It also indicates that growth in foodgrain production per capita -- a crude measure of improved food security -- was not positively correlated with increased commercialization over this

---

gross agricultural income was changed in 1985, when the value of output of village industry was re-assigned to industrial product. For the sake of consistency, 1983-84 gross agricultural income in each province was approximately adjusted to the post-1984 definition. Thus two sources of bias which give an exaggerated impression of the rate at which commercialization was proceeding have been removed.

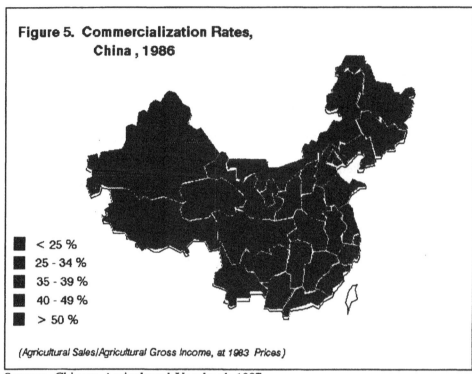

Figure 5. Commercialization Rates, China , 1986

< 25 %
25 - 34 %
35 - 39 %
40 - 49 %
> 50 %

(Agricultural Sales/Agricultural Gross Income, at 1983 Prices)

Source: Chinese Agricultural Yearbook 1987

period (in fact, there was little change in grain production nationwide in 1983-88). However, the provincial statistics are too aggregated to take us much beyond such simple generalities about trends.

Various factors, economic, political, and social have caused the regional disparity in promoting commercialization. Although the main restrictions on the market have been removed, the government still intervenes in the markets. The contract quotas of grains still accounted for the greatest volume of the total marketed grains. The grain market is still localized, and regional price variation is sizable. Markets for cash crops are relatively integrated since the government has unified cash crop prices with only slight regional differences and the largest portion of cash crops marketed is still purchased by government.

Inadequate rural infrastructure has been a constraint on the process of commercialization. In the remote areas, and especially in the mountainous areas, which are generally also poverty areas, transportation conditions, including road condition and density and vehicle density, is poor (Yan,). It is difficult for the local farmers to trade their products with those outside the region. Nationwide, about 50% of roads were unclassifiable, and 35% of roads were without asphalt, sand or stone pavement in 1984 (SSB, 1989).

C. Poverty Profile for China

1. Introduction

Poverty in the rural areas has been the major concern of the Chinese government in developing its economic reform policies. After a decade's success in economic reform, farmers' living standards have substantially improved (in terms of average income). However, the economic reforms have not benefited all households equally, and many farmers (or households) have remained in poverty.

By the end of 1985 there were an estimated 102 million rural residents (ten percent of the total population) whose net annual per capita incomes fell below the 200 yuan official poverty line, which was about one-half of the national average income in rural areas. Of these 40 million (four percent of the total population) had incomes below 150 RMB, at which it was difficult to maintain minimum subsistence

(OLGEDPA, 1989). However, by the end of 1988, based on the 1985 poverty line calculated in real terms, the poor population rose to 120 million, remaining at ten percent of the total population (RGCPA, 1990).

The distribution of the poor population shows considerable regionality, being concentrated in 22 provinces of western and central China as well as in the southwest border areas. A majority of impoverished areas are mountainous. In 1986, the Chinese government developed official poverty criteria, based on individual household income levels. In developing policy measures, however, it was easier to target administrative areas rather than individual households, for which only sample statistics were available. Therefore the poverty line was applied to entire counties rather than individual households. A total of 664 counties were identified as poor counties, of which 273 counties met criteria for national assistance and the remainder were to be assisted by the provinces. Special policies and programs were developed to assist these counties.

2. The Poverty Line and Its Determination

Drawing a poverty line is not a matter of simple calculation -- it involves political, financial and administrative considerations. A higher poverty line expands the official numbers of the poor population, which may entail high budgetary costs for subsidies. On the other hand, a lower line might exclude genuinely needy people. In a country where there is no reliable enumerated data on household welfare (only sample survey data), it is impractical to base a welfare program on the individual family's status; much easier to base it on geographic (administrative) area. Being poor qualifies one for welfare assistance from the government, and administrative units which are considered areas of poverty concentration may merit investment or consumption subsidies. There are advantages to being classified as poor. The selection of a poverty line is thus a political decision.

The Chinese Government Poverty Line in 1986

The newly-acknowledged poverty issue -- that certain regions remained poor after several years of the rural economic reform -- drew government's urgent attention. In 1986, the government attempted to designate "poor counties" in order to give these counties special assistance.

Thus ensued a process of determining a poverty line. The level of real income is used in most countries as the criterion of poverty. However, there are some exceptions, such as nutritional standards (used in India and Sri Lanka). Whatever indicator is used, a poverty line should measure the minimum requirement for subsistence or survival. In China, both per capita food consumption and net per capita income were taken into account in defining a poverty line.

The process had begun earlier in China with large-scale surveys of incomes and consumption conducted by the Rural Development Research Center (RDRC) of the State Council mainly in border provinces, inland mountainous and arid areas. Based on the survey assessment of minimal standards of living, in 1984 the poverty line was initially set at a net income of 120 yuan per capita and per capita grain consumption of 200 kg. Asked to enumerate the numbers of poor counties and the total poor population according to this criterion, local governments only reported 14 million poor households and a poor population of 70 million by early 1985. But when the central government decided to give financial assistance to the poor, local governments, not surprisingly, raised their estimates of the poor counties and populations to about 130 millions, ignoring the 120 yuan poverty line. Budgetary resources were limited, however, and it was agreed that the central government would determine the list of poor counties. The selection by RDRC of a poverty line of 200 yuan and 200 kg grain, and identification of counties containing 104 million poor, was finally designed to accommodate the numbers of eligible poor to the available budgetary resources (Zhu, 1992).

Based on this somewhat arbitrary poverty line (conveniently termed the "double two hundred"), the poor population, household, and county were developed as distinctive and equally arbitrary concepts:

(1) The population poverty line (200 yuan) is defined as an income level which can meet the expenditure requirements for basic needs, and a minimum nutritional standard.

(2) The household poverty line is defined as a family's expenses based on the population poverty line and a given family size.

(3) The county poverty line was designated slightly differently, by the criterion that 60% of households' per capita net income must fall below 150 yuan.

The Poverty Line Adjusted in 1988

Some further work on the criterion of a poverty line was undertaken by the State Statistical Bureau in 1989 and 1990. The research used the data from SSB's annual rural household survey (67,000 households). Two dimensions were used to measure the living standards of the poor: food consumption and daily expenses. Food consumption was based on a standard of nutritional intake prescribed by the CAN (2,400 KCal per capita; see below), while non-food consumption (cloth, fuel, housing, medicine, and miscellaneous), education and services were based on minimal standards. Physical consumption was converted to expenses at market prices. Based on this poverty line, the size of the poor population, numbers of poor households, and locations of poor areas were enumerated.

The Chinese Association of Nutrition (CAN) has recommended that the normal caloric intake of an male adult with light physical activities should be 2,400 KCal per day, based on WHO recommendations. Chinese farmers' caloric intake is mainly from grains and vegetables, and farm labor is their main daily activity, with a relatively high energy requirement. Therefore, 2,400 KCal intake was taken to be the poverty line in terms of nutritional standard. In fact, the energy intake of the rural poor (in income) in 1985 averaged 2,150 KCal (Zhu, 1992), while the national average daily energy consumption had already reached 2,641 KCal in 1983 (based on the survey of the Chinese Academy of Preventive Medical Sciences).

The 2,400 KCal figure theoretically applies to adult males, although soon the central government was treating it as a per capita energy intake. The figure is higher than Piazza's more elaborate estimate (taking into account body size, age, and sex composition of the population) of 2,270 KCal for all (not just rural) Chinese in 1982. Piazza's estimates increase by more than 100 KCal per decade as the population structure and average weight-for-age and height-for-age have grown.

According to suggestions by Chinese experts, the minimum living space per capita should be seven square meters based on human physiological requirements. For rural residents, an extra two square meters are required for storage. Therefore, the poverty line for housing was set at nine square meters, or about 53% of the current average housing area per capita in rural China (Jiang, 1990).

As for the remaining goods and services, it was necessary to distinguish "necessities" from luxury goods, where luxury goods are defined as having income elasticity greater than one. Subtracting expenditures on luxury goods from the commodity basket, the remaining expenses, on transportation, fuel, medical care, education, and entertainment, are a small component of total expenditure, which are still a legitimate part of minimum consumption requirements.

Working backwards from the above "real" consumption criteria to the approximately corresponding level of income, a poverty line for 1988 was derived as 260 yuan (see Annex III for details) (RGCPA, 1990).

However, the 1988 poverty line has not been used by government for any practical purposes; only for research purposes.

Determination of Poor Counties

The central government in 1986 determined the poverty line in terms of per capita income in the rural areas to be 200 yuan at 1985 prices. At the same time, for the purpose of determining the geographic scope of a poverty program, the official criteria for classification of counties as "poor" were established. Note that these criteria are not strictly objective (based on income levels), but rather define eligibility for administrative programs based partly on political considerations (favoritism for areas whose populations had been supportive during the Revolution, i.e., old revolutionary base areas; and of areas inhabited by cultural minority populations) and government financial resources. Three types of nationally-supported poor counties were distinguished:

(1) Counties entitled to special loans at subsidized interest rates:

- per capita net income below <u>150</u> yuan,

- incomes below <u>200</u> yuan for old revolutionary base areas and minority autonomous counties, and

- incomes between <u>200-300</u> yuan for counties which made a great contribution to the revolution, and some minority counties with special hardship.

(2) Pastoral areas entitled to special loans at subsidized interest rates:

- incomes below <u>300</u> RMB for the counties in pastoral areas,

- incomes below <u>200</u> RMB for semi-pastoral counties.

(3) Access to the "Sanxi" Special Fund:

- Counties in Hexi district and Dingxi district in Gansu and Xihaigu district in Ningxia.

A total of 301 counties fell into the above categories in 1986 (328 by 1988).

Besides state-supported poor counties, there were 363 (370 by 1988) counties designated as provincially-supported poor counties by the Office of Leading Group for Economic Development in Poor Areas (OLGEDPA). There was no standard poverty line for provincially-supported poor counties; generally the provincial governments made determination based on their financial situation.

As mentioned above, the poverty line of 200 yuan was not taken as the basis for defining poor counties, but rather a different standard was used. For administrative reasons, a geographic-based poverty line would be much easier for the central and provincial governments to deal with rather than a poverty line requiring evaluation of individual households. In addition, the strategy of poverty reduction is to assist regions to develop instead of individual families. Regionally-based projects, such as building roads, large-scale dams or irrigation systems, drinking water systems and so on, were carried out in designated poor areas. The disadvantage, however, was that those of the poor who do not live in designated poor areas could not benefit from the special poverty relief funds or grants.

Relationship among Three Poverty Lines

A yearly adjustment of the poverty line is needed due to inflation (RGCPA, 1990). By coincidence, the 1988 figure of 260 yuan evaluates at about 200 yuan in 1985 prices, so the results of objective estimation tend to confirm the outcomes of the earlier "political" process of poverty line determination.

In 1985, the poor population, whose net per capita income was below 200 yuan, or half of the national rural average level (398 yuan), was 102 million; the extremely poor population, whose net per capita income was below 150 yuan, totalled 40 million (OLGEDPA, 1989). By 1988, based on the poverty line of 260 yuan, the poor population was 120 million, poor households were 28.4 million, and the poor counties were 250 (RGCPA, 1990). On the other hand, if it is considered that all of the population of official poor counties benefit from special treatment or subsidies to a greater or lesser extent, then this population totalled 217 million in 1985.

3. Characteristics of Poverty

Historical Review

1949-1978 Period. Land reform in 1946-1949 for the first time provided land ownership rights to the poorest farmers, giving them a measure of food security and production incentives. However, these property rights were lost in 1958 following a series of institutional reforms which shifted the fundamental unit of production from the household to the mutual aid team, the producer's cooperative, and then the commune; although retrenchment in the 1960s shifted the locus of production and distribution back down to the level of the production team (around 10-50 households).

Under the commune system, as in other sectors of the economy, all production and marketing were brought within the state plan. The emphasis of planning on grain production, under the principle of "taking grain as the key link", eroded the farmers' ability to use their comparative advantage in growing cash crops. In areas, where the natural environment was not favorable to grain production, the yield of grain was too low to be profitable and sometimes insufficient to meet local demand for food.

Agricultural productivity (land and labor productivity) remained low until the 1970s, when modern technology (e.g., improved seed and chemical fertilizer) was introduced in better endowed areas, and brought about a "green revolution". In poorly-endowed areas, however, lack of capital, infrastructure (especially reliable irrigation), and knowledge hindered adoption of the new technology.

The government procurement system for agricultural products dominated the marketing of agricultural products. The obligatory procurement quota and low procurement prices were set by the government. In addition, the agricultural tax (land tax) was imposed on the commune, and paid in kind at rates differing regionally. These two compulsory payments formed a capital transfer supporting industrial development, which allowed the social accumulation (savings) rate to rise from 13.4-27.8% in 1958-78 (Zhu, 1992). The free market for agricultural products, especially grain, cotton, and edible oil, was prohibited. Commercial activities were not encouraged. In the poor areas, in any case, the farmers had little or no surplus after fulfilment of the government quota, taxes, and food consumption requirements, and the low level of quota prices provided them with essentially no cash income.

The income distribution system was based on work points earned by the production team members. Although in theory the system rewarded effort, in practice egalitarian principles resulted in little differences among team members in work points earned. The cash or commodity value of work points differed based on the production performance of each production team. The commune members were not allowed to engage in individual non-farming business as a source of supplementary income. Therefore the interhousehold income differential within a team was largely determined by the number of the laborers in a family, and the income differentials among teams, communes, and regions was far greater than that within a team.

Inadequate levels of food consumption was the another poverty issue arising from low incomes. From Figure 1 (Page 63 above), it is apparent that for a long period, the average Chinese farmers's consumption of grain fell below nutritional recommendations (2,400 KCal and 70 gm protein). A number of studies have suggested that the nutritional status of the Chinese farmers during this period (1950-1970) was 20% deficient in protein and 18% in energy. Zhou Binbin estimated that in 13-17 provinces, per capita food grain consumption was chronically below 210 kg (equivalent to 2,100 KCal). About 330-440 million people, representing 43-58% of the total population, were deficient in grain (cited by Zhu, 1992).

The Period of Economic Reform. The main thrust of rural economic reform was to increase the extent of commercialization of agriculture. Some of the previous relatively poor areas benefited from the new policies, specifically those areas with better natural endowment and geographic location, which were often able to increase cash crop production or diversify into off-farm activities.

However, the poverty areas which remained in 1986 clearly had not benefited substantially. First, the increase in procurement prices did not bring immediate profit to farmers who lacked viable alternatives to grain production, yet were unable to increase grain output due to low land productivity and low levels of adoption of modern inputs. Moreover, farmers who had no surplus over the combination of quota sales (before 1985) and self-consumption requirements could not benefit from substantially higher prices offered for sales above the quota. Although the opening of the free market provided an opportunity to develop commercial activities, some farmers either were too subsistence or barter oriented to engage in cash cropping, or were discouraged from the latter by food security concerns.

Engaging in non-farming business helped reduce rural underemployment and provided cash income earning opportunities. Such activities included industrial factories (basically processing of agricultural products or preliminary processing for urban industry), small scale mining (coal, lime) and construction materials, restaurants, shops, and services, such as construction or transport work. However, poor areas remaining in 1986 included those which had few opportunities for off-farm development, and/or lacked the capital, technology, and labor skills.

The Distribution of the Poor and Poor Counties

As mentioned above, the official 1985 (State Council) definition of "poor county" was based not only on per capita income, but also some political considerations. Therefore, the number of the poor counties exceeded the number qualified based only on income levels. However, the scope of poor counties as defined by the State Statistics Bureau in 1988 was limited to those with qualifying income levels. In both periods, the calculation of the poor population was based on family incomes nationwide, not the total population in the poor counties. Thus comparable statistics do indicate growth in poverty incidence: in 1985, the poor population was 102 million, or 12.2% of the total rural population; and by 1988, 120 million, or 13.9% of the total rural population (OLGEDPA, 1989).

In 1988, some 62.7% of the poor population lived in the northwest, the southwest, and the central-south regions. In the northwest, the poverty rate (percent of population under the poverty line) was 28.6%, the highest among regions. However, among provinces, Henan, which is not in the above regions, has the largest absolute number of the poor (17 million), 14.6% of the national total poor population, although its poverty rate at 25% was not the highest. Sichuan ranked second with 15 million poor. The poverty rate exceeded 20% in 11 provinces, among which Gansu had the highest rate (38.4%), Tibet was second (32.3%), and Shaanxi,

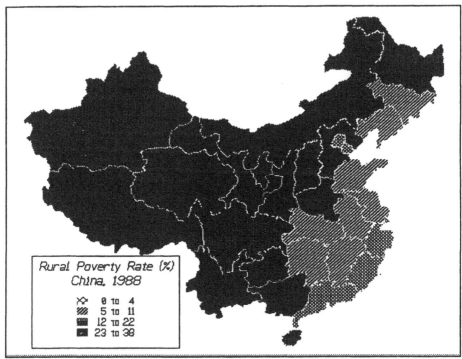

Figure 4. Rural Poverty by Province, 1988. Source: RGCPA, 1990.

Henan and Ningxia tied at about 25% (RGCPA, 1990).

The poor counties in 1985 were concentrated in 18 contiguous areas located in 22 provinces of central and western China; and mostly in mountainous areas (OLGEDPA, 1989). On the other hand, among the officially-designated poor counties (not based on poverty line calculations), 435 counties, about 62% of the total, are located in these 18 contiguous areas. In addition, about 75% of poor counties were located in the border areas, old revolutionary base areas and minority areas in 1988 (RGCPA, 1990).

A large proportion of the poor counties based on either definition are located in minority areas. Minority counties accounted for 43% of the 328 national-support poor counties (RGCPA, 1990). By 1988, there remained some 40% of the population in the poor minority counties living below the poverty line, of which about 70% were of minority nationalities (Zhu, 1992).

The Characteristics of the Poor Population and the Poor Areas

In characterizing and explaining poverty in China, the main focus must be on geographic differences, in view of the geographic concentration of poverty. The interhousehold poverty issue is not very significant, especially within a village (Zhu, 1992). This was because, in the dissolution of the communes, every household was leased an amount of land based mainly on the number of family members, and usually each household received a mix of plots of different quality so as to largely equalize the potential land productivity of each household within a village. Intervillage differences remain, due to differences in natural environment, human resources, and type of production. Some previously poor areas have escaped from poverty during the course of economic reform. However, overall regional disparity has not been reduced, but rather widened. In 1980, the average per capita income in 11 relatively poor provinces was 74% of that in 10 relatively developed provinces, while in 1985 this figure dropped to 65% (Zhu, 1992). The characteristics of the areas and populations which remain poor are described below.

Deteriorated Ecological Environment and Agricultural Production. As mentioned above, most of the poor are located in mountainous areas, such as the Loess Plateau, Qinghai-Tibet Plateau, or the Wuling and Taihang mountains.

Originally the quality of soil in these areas was poor and unfavorable for farming, and this has been worsened by long-term cropping without proper nutrient supplements. Deforestation (for land reclamation and fuel use) has caused severe soil erosion problems in these areas. In 1985, the cover rate of forest was 7.5% in eleven western provinces; in several of these --Gansu, Ningxia, Qinghai and Xinjiang -- it was 0.3-3.9%. The seriously eroded area within these provinces accounted for 67 million hectares, or 52% of the national total (Zhu, 1992). In plains areas, problem soils, such as red soils (e.g., in Jiangxi) and saline-alkaline soils (e.g., in the north China plain), prevail in most of the poor areas.

Water resources in the northwest are scarce. Annual precipitation is below 400 mm, ground water resources are also scanty and difficult to find due to depth. Availability of water is insufficient for human and animal consumption, not to mention irrigation. About 10 million people and 7 million animals are short of potable water (OLGEDPA, 1989).

Farming is the major production activity, and within farming, foodgrain production dominates. The low level of agricultural productivity and the need to meet subsistence requirements for food account for this; as do the government's "self-sufficiency" policy and the quota procurement system. because of the unfavorable production environment, grain yields in the poor counties were 58% of the national average level of grain in 1988. Yields in 279 poor counties located in the Loess Plateau and the areas between the eastern plains and western mountain areas were below 1.5 ton/ha, a figure about 40% of the national average. Due to shortage of capital, adoption rates of modern inputs are low. The application of chemical fertilizer in the poor areas was 34% lower than the national average of fertilizer use in 1986. The proportion of irrigated land was 32%, which was 14% lower than the national average level of irrigation land (OLGEDPA, 1989).

Inadequate Infrastructure. Inadequate infrastructure is one of the major obstacles to economic development in the poor areas. Poor transportation almost isolates the poor areas, especially the mountainous areas, and hinders development. In the west, which has an area two thirds of the national total, the length of railroads was less than a quarter of the national total. According to 1986 statistical data, 16% of the villages within the 664 poor counties were without access by road (OLGEDPA. 1989), compared to 6.5% nationwide (DASSSB, 1989). Such roads as exist are rarely all-weather roads. The isolation prevents such areas from exploiting such comparative advantages as exist, e.g., in mineral extraction or local specialties such as native herbs.

Poor communication and information systems are another aspect of the inadequate infrastructure. Some 22% of the villages in 664 poor counties lacked electricity. Telephone lines do not reach counties where even newspapers may be several days old (OLGEDPA, 1989).

After the economic reform, free markets, while legal, were still poorly developed in poor areas, due to isolation, poor transport, lack of tradable surpluses, and limited specialization.

Social Factors. Besides the economic factors, some social factors also relate to the poverty issue, all associated with human resources. A high population growth rate in poor areas has made it difficult to rise above poverty there, whereas declining population growth rates elsewhere permitted gains in per capita income. While the national average population growth rate fell from 2.84% to 1.12% between 1965 and 1985, in 11 western provinces it increased from 2.17% to 3.96%, ranging from 40-100% higher than the national average level. High population growth also created high dependent-to-laborer ratios (large family size). Sample data have shown there is a positive correlation between degree of poverty and family size (dependent population). The households with dependent ratios above three are more likely to be poor (Yan, 1990).

A high population growth is associated with a low quality of human resources. The national illiteracy rate was 21% in 1987, while it was 29% in 10 western provinces where the population growth rate was 2-3%. For a more extreme example, in Longlin Autonomous District, Guangxi Zhuanmg Autonomous Region, the illiteracy rate was 64.5%, while the population growth rate was 4.2% in 1981 (Yan, 1990). Technical training is largely lacking in the poor areas, leading to lack of understanding or acceptance of new technology.

Various locality-specific, usually water-borne diseases are common in the poor areas. A survey of 109 of the poorest counties revealed that major diseases of this sort prevailed in 94 counties. The medical care system in the poor areas is also measurably weaker than elsewhere in the rural areas, although the degree of regional inequality is not extraordinary. There were 22 hospital beds per 10,000 persons in the 11 western provinces, 9% lower than the national average; and the number of technical medical personnel per capita, at 30 per 10,000, was 7% lower than the national average (OLGEDPA, 1989). These figures do not fully reflect the more substantial gap in quality of personnel and facilities.

A long-term poverty state results in low quality of human resources. Even if natural resources are favorable, the poor lack confidence in their ability to bootstrap themselves out of poverty through commercialization (Wang and Bai, 1987). Even local cadres, who play the fundamental role in the implementation of poverty alleviation policies and programs, such as educating the labor force and demonstrating and promoting adoption of advanced techniques, are not well-educated. At the village level, 11% of cadres were illiterate (RIRDCASS, 1991).

The Office of Leading Group of Economic Development in Poor Areas's study (1989) based on a survey of 417 households in four poor provinces (Gansu, Guizhou, Inner Mongolia and Hebei) has shown that there is some relationship between resource endowment and poverty state: (i) negative correlation between labor endowment and income, (ii) positive correlation between the educational level of the head of household and income, (iii) households mainly engaged in cropping were the poorest in the poor areas, (iv) low land productivity in grain production kept the households at bare self-sufficiency, and (v) the commercial rate was very low in the poor areas. In Guizhou, for example, the marketing rate for grains was 12%, and the resale rate was 17% in 1988.

On average, the consumption expenditures of the poor were 22-54% in excess of their net income. As direct grants in aid from the central government appear to represent only about 6% of per capita net income, much of the remainder must represent net borrowing or dissaving. As the poor are in no position to borrow or dissave continuously, the recorded net borrowing or dissaving of the poor probably reflects the movement of some households temporarily into the poverty class because of poor harvests, natural disasters, or other transitory conditions (such households would be expected to repay loans when conditions returned to normal).

Despite dissavings, expenditures on consumption were also lower than the national average by 47%. As one would expect, the gap was smallest in proportion for food (with a low income elasticity of demand) and highest for housing and miscellaneous. The details are shown in Table 3.4:

Table 3.1. Comparison of Living Expenditure of the Poor and Non-poor

	Expend. of the poor (yuan) I	Expend. of the national average (yuan) II	Difference (II-I)/II(%)
Total	255	477	46.5
1.Consumer goods	241	450	46.4
Food	162	255	36.5
Clothing	23	41	45.1
Housing	16	71	76.9
Fuel	16	22	27.6
Miscellaneous	25	61	56.6
2.Services Expenditure	14	27	48.7

Source: RGCPA. 1990.

4. Food Security in the Poor Areas

As it mentioned above, that China's food security issue was basically solved in the 1980s. However, many of the poor counties have a food security problem due to low agricultural productivity as well as poor transport access.

Although cultivated land per capita in poor counties is close to or above the national average (0.13 ha per capita), agricultural yields are low due to poor soil and moisture endowments and low input levels. Based on a sample of 663 poor counties, in 1987 the average grain yield in poor areas was 183 kg., about 76% of the national average. Poor counties in five provinces averaged yields lower than 100 kg. The irrigated area averaged 32% of total cultivated area in poor counties, compared to 46% nationwide. Chemical fertilizer use per hectare in poor areas was 33% lower than the national average (OLGEDPA, 1989).

As a result of low levels of productivity, based on 664 poor-county data, grain production per capita in poor counties averaged 328 kg. in 1987, while the national average was 380 kg. Poor counties in Gansu had the lowest level, 150 kg., while in eight provinces, poor counties produced under 300 kg. per capita.

Roughly estimating (based on data of 664 poor county) per capita grain availability as production minus procurement plus resales (which omits purchases of grain from outside), in 1983 there were 46 counties (about 7% of the total) with availability below 200 kg (the mean was 161 kg). Availability in about 25% of counties (168) ranged between 200-300 kg (mean 251 kg). That is, about 32% of poor counties appeared to be deficit in grain consumption, unless they had the means

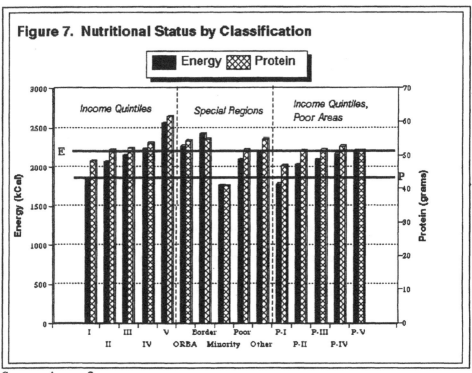

Figure 7. Nutritional Status by Classification

Source: Annex 2.

to import grain from elsewhere (in which case, one would not want to consider them "food insecure").

In 1987, the situation had worsened compared to 1983: about 49% of the poor counties were deficit in grain consumption on the above measure. Of deficit counties, there were 84 counties (about 12.7% of the total) where grain availability average only 164 kg.

Does the presence of a food deficit indicate a food insecurity problem? Is the criterion of "poor counties" an adequate way to identify the food insecure? Is food insecurity the primary characteristic of poverty in China? Analysis of 1988 sample rural household data (for 10,000 households) suggests that the answer to all three questions may be negative, if we are speaking of chronic food insecurity (Figure 7).[9] It is instructive to compare nutritional status when the sample is divided in three different ways: (a) by income quintiles for the sample as a whole; (b) for regions identified as special targets (representing some 30% of the sample), i.e., "old revolutionary base areas", border areas, minority areas, poor counties, and all other areas (note that the special area categories overlap, and the statistics presented for each area do not exclude overlaps in classification); and (c) by income quintiles for households in poor counties (20% of the sample).

It is evident that all but the top quintile of farm households experienced at least marginally food insecurity (energy intake below 2,250 KCal per capita); but each quintile in the poor counties falls only a few percent below the corresponding quintile for the rural population as a whole. When we compare the mean intakes for poor areas with "other" (i.e., non-special areas), the difference is also relatively small. In fact, minority areas, not poor areas, appear to have the most serious chronic food security problem. This suggests that the criterion for "poor counties" is not a very good identifier of chronic food insecurity, even if food deficits exist (perhaps because enough food flows into these areas to make up the deficit). However, as discussed

---

[9] Energy and protein consumption was estimated from major food groups (Annex A.II). Only milk, fruit, alcohol were omitted, which may have accounted for well under 50 kCal per capita per day. Our estimates are significantly below some other estimates made from approximate national food balance sheets, but that is because survey-estimated rural per capita food consumption is substantially lower than estimates of total (rural and urban) per capita consumption based on official production statistics. See Piazza (1987) for a discussion of this fact.

above, poor areas usually have environmental and infrastructure handicaps which may cause serious <u>intertemperal</u> food insecurity.

Also, the degree of inequality in food consumption associated with income inequality is surprisingly small. Even though the poorest one-fifth of the rural population was certainly food insecure and the richest one-fifth certainly not, the extent of inequality in food consumption in China is much less than inequality of income. Food insecurity thus may not be as important a characteristic of poverty as other deficiencies (education, health, non-food consumer goods, etc.).

In general, the food security issue in China has been solved on average after the decade-long economic reform. As China lacks a landless rural population, there is no large segment of the population which is desperately food insecure, and food deficit areas are able to import food from other provinces. However, regional and inter-household food insecurity still persists, especially in the poor areas where the natural resource endowment is not favorable to agriculture and rural infrastructure, especially transportation, is inadequate. Some degree of food insecurity is likely to remain as long as poverty exists in the poor areas.

5. Policy for Poverty Alleviation

Equalizing class differential was one of the initial goals in establishing the People's Republic. Assisting the poorest people to escape from poverty has been a long-term concern. Earlier policies and programs included major social welfare programs, not focused on regional development but on relief for the individual poor.

The Ministry of Civil Administration administered a relief fund to assist poor households. The communes were responsible for taking care of the "five guarantee households" (wubao hu), who included the elderly, weak, and disabled, and spouses and parents of absent or dead soldiers. These people were assured of food, clothing, fuel, housing, medical care and burial expenses. Resale of grain from the government was intended for households who were deficit of grain, although the amounts were not guaranteed to offset the deficit. Medical care was based on the cooperatives, which subsidized medical expenses and provided paramedical "bare-foot doctors" to give simple medical treatment.

However, these programs of poverty alleviation, described as a "blood transfusion", failed to reach the expected result (Zhu, 1992) because they only helped the poor to overcome temporary difficulties, targeted consumption rather than production, and encouraged dependence on government relief. They failed in particular to help the poor to build up their own economic capacity. This led government to reconsider the poverty alleviation policies, the fundamental change in poverty alleviation policy in the 1980s was from "blood transfusion" to "blood making", i.e., from subsidizing living standards to targeted public investment and production subsidy. The new policy encouraged the poor to establish their own capacity to develop the economy, from basic improvement in the ecological environment (e.g., growing grass and trees, watershed conservation) to promotion of commercialization (encouraging long-distance trading, diversifying agricultural production and establishing rural non-farm enterprises) (OLGEDPA, 1989).

In early 1980s, the central government established a special fund to assist the "Sanxi" areas, where poverty was most severe and the ecological environment was seriously degraded. The establishment of this fund drew government attention to the poverty issue. At the meeting of the National People's Congress in 1986, poverty alleviation was put on the agenda of the Seventh Five-Year Plan.

In 1986, the Leading Group for Economic Development of Poor Areas under the State Council was established. This Leading Group is specially charged with making and monitoring the implementation of policies and programs for poverty alleviation. The current policy and programs are targeted to assist poor areas to build their own capacity to improve the current poverty situation and food security problem. Besides the annual relief fund and resale grain, a number of special projects and programs have been made to assist poor counties through special poverty-relief funds and low-interest loans. Thereafter, a special fund of 4.05 billion yuan for economic development in the poor areas was appropriated annually. Of this fund, 25% is for public investment and grants, and the remainder being low-interest loans and credit. These funds are not to be used for relief, but rather for special rural infrastructure projects and projects to restore the ecological environment.

In 1985-87, public works (with payment in kind) projects (with grain, cotton, and cotton cloth as means of payment) building roads, tunnels, bridges, irrigation and drinking water systems have improved rural infrastructure in poor areas. In 1990, one of the public works projects sought to create stable-yield fields (bao chan tian) in ecologically-degraded areas on a scale of one mu (0.06 ha) per capita, in order to guarantee subsistence. These public works not only provide the poor with employment opportunities, but also improve rural infrastructure, such as roads, reservoirs, and drinking water systems. To date, this program has shown great accomplishments in substantially improving transportation (roads and bridges), irrigation systems (reservoirs), and drinking water systems in the poor areas. One of the notably successful cases involved improvements to the transport system in Guizhou province (Guizhou, 1989).

In order to facilitate economic development in the poor areas, the government also provides production inputs, e.g., fertilizer, plastic sheets, timber, and trucks, at subsidized prices.

In 1985, contract procurement replaced quota procurement in rural China. In the poor areas, the state reduced or exempted the agricultural tax for a 3-5 year period. From 1987, the nationally-supported poor areas were exempted from transfer of depreciation funds for energy and transportation and the reserve requirements for banks in such areas were reduced. The provincial governments correspondingly took measures favorable to the poor areas, such as reduction or exemption from procurement contracts and the business tax on township enterprises. (At the same time, it should be noted that energy and mineral production are among the major sources of income in poor areas such as Gansu or Shanxi, yet administered pricing has held the prices of such primary products well below market value.)

The central government has also sought to mobilize other forms of social assistance to the poor areas. This includes (1) loans or transfers of skilled personnel and transfers of technology, e.g., through establishment of joint ventures between enterprises in developed and backwards areas; (2) migration of population in the poor areas to other areas either building some new villages or merging in some low man-land ratio areas.

Problems of Policy Implementation: These anti-poverty policies and programs have had some successes, particularly the public works and productive investment programs (Guizhou, 1989). However, some implementation problems have been noted. In particular, evaluation and appraisal of projects has been inadequate, due partly to lack of statistical data allowing targeting of project performance and assessment of impacts. Coordination of the various projects has been weak, as anti-poverty funds have been disbursed through various ministries and passed down through administrative channels to local governments. The coordinating role of the Leading Group has been minimal once project funding has been approved (Zhu, 1992). An effective monitoring system has also been lacking, and implementation has depended on inexperienced or poorly trained local administrators. As a result, up to 1990, about 35% of projects were in default on loans (mostly for poorly conceived or managed industrial projects). Without effective monitoring, adjustments or corrections mid-course have not been made.

6. Conclusions

The poverty issue is perceived as a new challenge to the Chinese government. It is not only an economic issue, but also involves social and political questions. Since 1986, the Chinese government has been making great efforts, financial and technical, to assist the officially-defined poor areas. The major policy change which occurred in the 1980s was to encourage commercialization in order to build the ability of the poor to climb out of poverty. The projects and programs for poverty alleviation undertaken have had a great effect on the poor areas. However, there are still some obstacles to commercialization and food security. Improving rural infrastructure and promoting adoption of modern technology in the poor areas are the crucial measures for the government to consider.

D. The Characteristics of Rural China

The Chinese Farm Household

Chinese households became independent production units again after 1983, four years after the beginning of the economic reform. As in other developing countries, the Chinese rural household is a unified body of producer and consumer. The nuclear family is the predominant form in rural China (roughly 70% of rural families, the remainder being extended families). Most household heads are male. The average family size is almost five persons, and families with 4-6 people are 70% of the total (UCR-CASS). About 30% of the population is under 16 in age, and 45% between 16-40. The average labor force size per family is about 2.9 persons, varying between one and five.   Every household has several plots of land held under a 15-year government lease (starting in 1983). The farm size is quite variable regionally: the average land area per farm household in 1988 was 0.77 ha, ranging by province from 2.5 ha in Heilongjiang Province to as little as 0.24 ha in Zhejiang

Province (UCR-CASS). In China, all natural resources (land, forests, mines, lakes,

and rivers) are state owned, and private property rights in natural resources are

forbidden. Therefore, there is no formal land market. However, in some (well-

developed) areas, non-farming households rent their land out, most keeping a piece

of land to grow grain for their own consumption and contract quota sales; and a few

households have completely given up farming and become pure food purchasers.

Conversely, a few so-called "specialized households" effectively sublease land from

other households, although the officially-approved approach is to assume the

contractual rights and obligations of other households for compensation and with

official approval.

Possession of production assets, such as medium and small-size tractors,

combines, storage buildings, draft animals, agricultural, industrial and transport

machinery, and other equipment and tools, also varies regionally. In the 1988 sample

data, the lowest level of assets was found in Sichuan Province, where each household

averaged 665 yuan of productive assets; whereas the highest was in Qinghai Province

with an average of 3,040 yuan. In general, provinces where households have over

1,000 yuan of production assets are those where state farms were common in the

past, the land/labor ratio is high, and the degree of mechanization in farming

exceeds other areas. Machinery and other fixed assets were assigned to households

at the time of dissolution of the state farms.

The households have trivial amounts of liquid capital for their production. Formal credit (through the Rural Credit Cooperatives) has existed for some time and an informal credit market is just emerging. Bank loans and credit are now available for individuals, but about one-third of farmers regard themselves as credit-constrained, due mainly to savings levels which do not meet minimum deposit requirements (Feder et al., 1991). Formal credit is mainly used for production (above 90%). In lieu of land as collateral, credit was previously offered against guarantees by the communes, and currently requires township government guarantees. Informal loans or credit, primarily from relatives and friends without interest, are used mainly for non-productive activities, like funeral ceremonies.

Although the fact that about 45% of China's cultivated area is under irrigation helps to stabilize crop yields, the monsoonal climate, relative concentration of rainfall in the summer season, prevalence of multiple cropping, dependence of upland areas on rainfall conditions, etc. all lead to considerable local yield variation; hence production risk is likely to be a prominent consideration among farmers.

A general statistical description of the agricultural sector points up the overall dependence on crop growing as the primary farm activity, and of grain as the primary crop: about 78.5% of total rural labor was engaged in farming, of which 83% was in cropping (grain and cash crops) in 1988. Crops accounted for more than 60% of the gross value of farming, within which foodgrains occupied 64%. Livestock is the next largest activity, accounting for 21% (DASSSB, 1989). According to official farm household surveys, some 83% of net rural household income is attributable to family production activity (the remainder is mainly wage earnings and transfers), of which 49% was from farming, 18.6% from livestock production, and the rest from household-based non-farming or off-farm activities (SSB, 1989).

Regional disparities in the distribution of income remain significant, due mainly to productivity differentials. In the well-developed coastal areas (e.g., Jiangsu, Shanghai, Guangdong), average incomes are 3-4 times those in the underdeveloped areas (e.g., Heilongjiang, Gansu, Shaanxi). However, within provinces, the degree of inequality is not very significant: in the 1988 sample data, the Gini ratio ranged from a maximum of 0.394 in Tianjin to 0.222 in Shanghai. Nationwide, there were ten provincial units with Gini ratios above 0.3, and the remainder fell between 0.222-0.299; none fell below 0.2 in 1988 (Khan et al., 1992). In the developed areas, the income share from non-farming activities was dominant, while in the underdeveloped areas, farming was the dominant income source. Varying rates of commercialization of agriculture is another factor explaining the income gap.

Interhousehold income differentials are sensitive to the type of business in which the household is engaged. The highest incomes are among the owners and managers of private enterprises, and of course non-farm households have higher income than farm households (Kuhn, 1992).

The household labor force size and dependency ratio (dependents/workers) are demographic factors which affect the income of the households. Poor households usually have less workers and higher dependency ratios.

The farmers allocate their income between production investment and consumption. Since we focus on the relationship among food security, poverty and commercialization in a static context, discussion of savings and productive investment is omitted, as also it is neglected in the mathematical models. Farmers do in fact save part of current income for future use either in production or consumption. Savings patterns are similar to those found in other developing or developed economies across income levels: negative for lower income groups, and rising to proportions of 20-30% for the top decile of the farm household income distribution.

Market System

The prevalence of market risk in post-reform rural China has not been well-studied, due partly to data limitations. With a large proportion of staple food marketed through government channels, and a history of unreliable official administration of foodgrains distribution (which focused mainly on a few urban areas), farmers have had good reason to fear that the market could not provide grain when needed at reasonable prices, and have therefore been supposed to pursue "safety first" strategies. Figure 8 presents some fragmentary monthly price series from major rural markets in selected provinces (deflated by official indices of prices of industrial goods sold in the rural areas). While a general uptrend in free market grain prices prevailed during the period (in excess of the trend in quota prices), substantial and sometimes sudden fluctuations around these trends can be seen. Even though farmers could count on selling most of their grain and cash crop

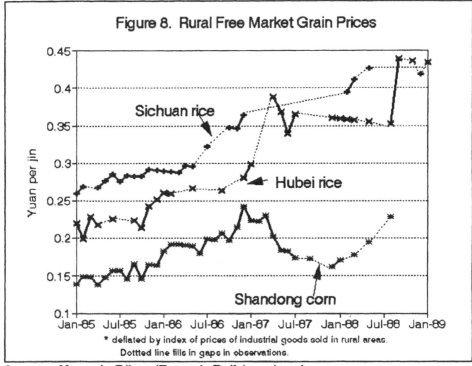

Figure 8. Rural Free Market Grain Prices

* deflated by index of prices of industrial goods sold in rural areas.
Dottted line fills in gaps in observations.

Sources: Nongmin Ribao (Farmer's Daily), various issues.

production to government procurement organs at relatively stable and predictable prices, sales of surpluses faced some degree of price risk (for markets outside of major commercial production areas, probably greater than indicated in the figure).

A land tax is still imposed, previously paid only in kind (grain), but currently either in grain or cash. The quantity of land tax is fixed for several years based on average yields, hence has no effect on marginal production incentives. In addition, previous "contributions" to the collective, such as to the accumulation fund or social welfare fees, may still be required by the township government.

The market for inputs, especially manufactured inputs, e.g., chemical fertilizer, machinery, and fuel, is controlled by the state through state commercial enterprises and the supply and marketing cooperatives. There are two prices for these inputs -- the (lower) list price and the market price. The list price is for planned supply (amounts supplied to each area are fixed) and for exchange for agricultural products (e.g., for sale of livestock products and cash crops). The market price applies to non-planned supply. Based on the 1988 **UCR-CASS** survey, the proportions purchased at list prices for various commodities were roughly: chemical fertilizer, pesticides, and water pumps one-third; diesel oil 50%; gasoline for production use 25%; and other production materials, such as plastic sheets, 20-25%.

A rural casual labor market has been developing since the early 1980s, with little government interference. This is due partly to the shift of labor to non-farming activities (in 1978, 90% of the total rural labor force was primarily engaged in farming, and this fell to 79% by 1990 (DASSSB, 1985-1991)), partly to a certain degree of consolidation of farms in the hands of "specialized households", and mostly to unequal distribution of land relative to family labor forces. However, most farms are very small, with landholdings capable of being worked by a family labor force with at most a little assistance from friends or relatives at harvest time.

The relaxation of restrictions on marketing has encouraged farmers to increase their commercial activities. Urban free markets of agricultural products as well as rural periodical markets provide an outlet for surplus production and source of supplementary food and non-food consumer goods and production inputs.

Although rural markets in some areas tend to be localized and restrictions on interprovincial trade in major agricultural products (especially staple foods) remain, interregional private wholesale trade has been growing.

The share of purchased food in the farmers' diet has been increasing since 1978, when it was 24%. It was about a half of the total food consumption by 1988 (SSB, 1990). Within purchased foods, staple foods (grain or grain-based products) represented less than 10%. Among non-food consumption, fuel was the least dependent on cash purchases, whereas clothing, housing and miscellaneous commodities all are more than 98% purchased (SSB, 1983-1990).

From the above discussion, it is apparent that the post-reform Chinese rural economy shares many characteristics of farm economies in other developing countries, including prevalence of production and market risk. However, the following particular characteristics of the Chinese rural farm economy should be taken into account in constructing models of farmer behaviour:

(a) incomplete markets in land, farm labor, and capital (with growth in market activity, licit or illicit, over the 1980s);

(b) dual or parallel product and material input markets, with purchases and sales at low administered (quota or list) prices and higher negotiated or market prices (with growth over the 1980s to dominance of transactions concluded at free market and negotiated prices);

(c) <u>marginal</u> prices for both inputs and products generally being market prices by the late 1980s (because of fixed sales quotas and fixed or limited allocations of inputs at subsidized list prices); and

(d) geographically-localized free markets in staple foods, especially outside of the coastal deltas. Furthermore, the less poor and the more commercialized the area within China, the more complete and integrated the markets are likely to be, that is, the less market imperfections or incompleteness are likely to influence farm decision making.

IV. The Empirical Chinese Agricultural Household Model

A. Previous Empirical Studies of Chinese Agricultural Household Models

Applications of agricultural household models to Chinese rural households have mainly explored the impact of government restrictions and/or collective farming institutions in the pre-reform period. For example, Terry Sicular (1986) used household models to test the effects of marketing restrictions (either procurement quota or free market prohibitions) on labor allocation on a Chinese collective farm (i.e., production team of the People's Commune) in 1979. A linear program was used to characterize production decision making, and a comparison of basic (restricted) and unrestricted solutions was employed to test the effect of planning restrictions on the team's income, production pattern and labor allocation. The model assumed the absence of a labor market, the existence of a state monopoly on all procurements, and that the team acted like a household making joint decisions on production and consumption. The production level and input (including labor) utilization, land use pattern, and profit level of the team, as predicted from the restricted model, fit observed behaviour better than the unrestricted model. Three constraints originating in government policy -- forced cotton growing, hog marketing, and vegetable oil self-sufficiency, were binding, influencing the team's behaviour and labor allocation. Quota procurement requirements for grain proved to have no impact (if only because markets other than state procurement were ignored).

Two applications of farm models to post-reform rural China were developed by Feder et al. (1990 and 1991) to explore the effects of credit markets on farmers' production and consumption, and the impact of uncertainty of land rights on farm investment behaviour, respectively. In both cases, a simple two-period household model was constructed encompassing farm household consumption, production, and investment. In the credit-oriented model, household utility from two-period consumption was maximized, with the future stream of consumption represented by the value of future capital, and with constraints on production, consumption, capital flow, and budget. Credit availability was assumed to affect current production (variable input purchase), and thereby consumption and investment for the future. The optimal solutions were shown to be dependent on credit availability (whether supply of credit is greater or less than demand). Whether or not the household can borrow the desired amount or is constrained by upper limits on credit availability determines separability. The empirical results indicated that production is affected by land, capital, education and farmer experience when credit is unconstrained, while if credit is constraining, only land has a positive impact on supply of output.

In the land rights model, farmers are assumed to choose between investment in farm production and housing, where housing services appear also in the utility function. Future composite consumption is specified to be either determined by income resulting from farm production, or, if land is taken away from the farmer, future income is a fixed compensatory payment. The existence of non-zero probability of each of these outcomes introduces uncertainty to the model, and, on the restrictive assumption of an additive, separable utility function (in commodities and housing for each period), the comparative statics implies that investment in farm production (with uncertain results) responds negatively to increased risk of land confiscation, as the farmer, of course, chooses instead to invest in housing. Econometric tests on cross-sectional survey data (using dummy variables to assess farmers' sense of tenure security) indeed indicated that farmers' production investment decisions were mainly determined by a combination of tenure security perception, farm size, and credit availability.

Overall, then, the two previous empirical applications of household models to rural China above suffer from either a pre-reform focus (Sicular) or a narrow purpose (Feder et al.), and provide us little guidance besides indicating that such models can be usefully applied to Chinese data.

B. The Household Models

1. Chinese Agricultural Household Models

In this section, we intend to explore several variations on agricultural household models applicable to China. For our purposes -- in particular, to establish the framework for econometric analysis -- a basic household model is sufficient. However, several variations on this model need to be explored to be sure that the basic model does not contribute to misleading conclusions for the Chinese case.

Basic Model

In developing a basic model of Chinese agricultural households, we assume that

- Chinese agricultural households are semi-commercial farmers, and both producers and consumers; there is a geographically-integrated product market with government interventions, such as sales quotas;

- All households are price-takers in the market;

- The technology state is constant, and production is characterized by constant returns to scale;

- Production inputs include only labor and land (other purchased inputs are temporarily ignored for simplification);

- Households are engaged in farming and non-farming activities. Farming activities include growing a staple crop and a cash crop;

- Labor or land markets are non-existent (due to official prohibition); and

- Labor-leisure choices are ignored [10].

- Family assets (endowment): labor and land, which are allocated among two farm production activities -- food and cash crops;

- Marketing: market sale of food equals production minus own-consumption; cash crops are all sold;

- Market purchases: may include food and a composite non-food commodity;

---

[10] If incorporated, leisure would become an additional argument in the utility function. This has the effect of destroying recursiveness of production-consumption decisions, and complicating solutions with extra terms (Strauss 1986). Ignoring substitution between leisure and commodities is a useful simplification, and very reasonable for Chinese farmers. As Chinese experts speak of one-third of the rural labor force as being "surplus", the marginal utility of leisure is probably very low.

These assumptions are expressed mathematically as follows:

MAX $U = U(C_f, C_n, Z)$, $U' > 0$, $U'' < 0$.   {Utility function}

Subject to

(1.1) $P_f(F_f - C_f) + P_c F_c + E = C_n P_n$ {Budget constraint}

where $F_f - C_f > 0$ $=>$ net sale

$F_f - C_f < 0$ $=>$ net purchase

(1.2) $F(F_f, L_f, A_f) = 0$ {Production function, food}

(1.3) $G(F_c, L_c, A_c) = 0$ {Production function, cash crop}

(1.4) $L_f + L_c = \bar{L}$ {Labor endowment}

(1.5) $A_f + A_c = \bar{A}$ {Land endowment}

where C_f consumption of food

C_n consumption of non-food

Z parameter reflecting family composition (size), such that

$$\frac{\partial U_{C_f}}{\partial z} > 0$$

P_f market price of food

P_c market price of cash crops

F_f food crop production

F_c cash crop production, all marketed

L_f labor allocated on food crop production

L_c labor allocated on cash crop production

A_f land used on food crop production

A_c land used on cash crop production

P_n market price of non-food

$\bar{L}$ total family labor

$\bar{A}$ total farm land

E   Exogenous income, e.g., gifts, government relief funds, etc., introduced as a device useful in later analysis for indicating income effects

The household maximizes its utility of consumption of food and non-food goods subject to a production function and income constraints with exogenous fixed prices and resource endowments. The recursive property holds, that is, the household makes its production decisions before its consumption decisions. As E is entirely exogenous, variations in income depend entirely on profits from farm production.

In order to explore the household's decision-making process and relationships among output, input, and consumption, the first and second order conditions are derived as follows:

The Lagrangian function can be written with the utility function as maxim, and the income constraint (equation 1.1) and two production functions for food and cash crops (combining 1.2-1.4), each with multipliers representing the marginal utility deriving from relaxation of the corresponding constraints:

(1.6) $\mathcal{L} = U(C_f, C_n, Z) + \lambda[P_f(F_f\text{-}C_f) + P_cF_c + E - P_nC_n]$

$$+ \ \mu[F(F_f, \ L_f, \ A_f)] \ + \ \phi[G(F_c, \ \bar{L}\text{-}L_f, \ \bar{A}\text{-}A_f)]$$

The first and second order conditions (1.7 and 1.8), assuming that an interior solution

exists, are given in the Mathematical Annex (Annex I). As the Hessian (1.8) is block

diagonal, the system is recursive: the effects of inputs, outputs and output prices on

consumption decisions are entirely due to the profit effect, and income, preferences,

and price of consumption commodities do not affect the production decision. (This

separability property holds with either the existence of labor markets, or without

labor markets if leisure is not an argument in the utility function. In this model, total

labor is thus a fixed factor, although the proportions used in production of each crop

are variable.)

This basic model does not explicitly identify gross quantities of food

marketed or purchased -- only the net surplus or deficit of food production over

consumption. However, as there is no advantage to sell food and then buy it back

at the same price, we can assume that the farmer does not sell what he intends to

consume, and then consider the effect of price variation on production, consumption,

and market surplus.

Crop production, whether food or cash crop, responds positively to a

change in own-price, i.e. $\partial F_i / \partial p_i > 0$ owing to the quasi-convex production function

(Strauss, 1986). Staple food price increases have a negative substitution effect on

consumption, and a positive income effect weighted by the net market surplus. If the

farmer is a net purchaser of food ($F_f - C_f < 0$), the effect of increased price on consumption, from the Hessian matrix (third row of 1.8 in Annex I), will be unambiguously negative.

$$(1.9) \quad \frac{\partial C_f}{\partial P_f} = \frac{\partial C_f}{\partial P_f}\Big|_U + (F_f - C_f)\frac{\partial C_f}{\partial Y} \quad \text{where Y represents total income}[11].$$

The consumption of market-purchased goods is positively influenced by the cash crop price through the income effect.

$$(1.10) \quad \frac{\partial C_n}{\partial P_c} = F_c \frac{\partial C_n}{\partial Y}$$

In this basic model, the farmer makes his production decision simply based on profit-maximization. He follows his comparative advantage given his fixed endowment of labor and land. The comparative advantage is influenced by the price ratio of food and cash crops, and the relative productivities of land in each crop, i.e.,

$$(1.11) \quad \frac{P_f}{P_c} = \frac{\mu}{\varphi}\frac{F_F}{G_C}$$

Regarding the commercialization process, this model does not clearly indicate how the farmer will react to an exogenous food price increase: the response of marketed surplus of food crop to own-price change is clearly positive if the farmer

---

[11] Note that total (endogenous plus exogenous) income, $Y = P_f(F_f - C_f) + P_c F_c + E$. E represents exogenous income.

is a net purchaser, but ambiguous in sign if the farmer is a net seller. The total effect is:

$$(1.12) \qquad \frac{\partial (F_f - C_f)}{\partial P_f} = (\frac{\partial F_f}{\partial P_f} - \frac{\partial C_f}{\partial P_f})|_u + (F_f - C_f)(\frac{\partial F_f}{\partial Y} - \frac{\partial C_f}{\partial Y})$$

The first two terms hold utility constant, and comprise a substitution effect, which is clearly positive. The last terms comprise the income effect, which is negative if marketed surplus is positive and food is a normal good.

The results above shed little immediate light on the relationship among poverty, food security, and commercialization. To examine the latter, we need to define these in terms consistent with our model. For example, **poverty** may be treated by examining the impact of exogenous variations in wealth, for example, taking A, the family endowment of the fixed production asset (in this two-factor model, land), as a simple indicator of wealth. **Food security**, if measured as an endogenous outcome of choice, is a difficult concept to model mathematically, food consumption can be used as a proxy for it. Thus, it is better to settle on Z, the parameter in the utility function reflecting family size and composition, as a proxy for food requirements. **Commercialization** may be measured as a commercial rate:

$$(1.13) \quad R = [(F_f - C_f)P_f + F_c P_c]/[F_f P_f + F_c P_c] = 1 - [C_f P_f /(F_f P_f + F_c P_c)]$$

i.e., total net sales (food and cash crops) divided by total value of production.

The **relationship between poverty and commercialization** $\frac{\partial R}{\partial A}$ can be

seen to depend strictly on the income elasticity of demand for the food commodity,

C_f, that is, to depend on properties of the family utility function:

Letting $Y = F_f P_f + F_c P_c$, the sign of $\frac{\partial R}{\partial A}$ is the reverse of the sign of

(1.14)

$$
\frac{\partial\left[P_f \frac{C_f}{Y}\right]}{\partial A} = \frac{P_f\left[\frac{\partial C_f}{\partial Y}\frac{\partial Y}{\partial A}Y - \frac{\partial Y}{\partial A}C_f\right]}{Y^2} = \frac{P_f\left[\frac{\partial C_f}{\partial Y}Y - C_f\right]\frac{\partial Y}{\partial A}}{Y^2} = \frac{P_f\left[\frac{\partial C_f}{\partial Y} - \frac{C_f}{Y}\right]\frac{\partial Y}{\partial A}}{Y}
$$

which depends on whether the income elasticity of demand for food

$$
\eta_{C_f} = \frac{\partial C_f}{\partial Y}\frac{Y}{C_f} \overset{>}{\underset{<}{\gtrless}} 1
$$

Since the common <u>empirical</u> finding (Tsakok, 1990) is that the income elasticity of

demand for food (especially staple food) is less than one, we would expect that **cross-**

sectionally commercial rates would increase with increased land endowment (and so

also with wealth and income).

The relationship $\frac{\partial R}{\partial Z}$ is straightforward only if the model is separable

(recursive), so that production is not affected by consumption (or any parameters of the utility function). $\dfrac{\partial U_{C_f}}{\partial Z} > 0 \rightarrow \dfrac{\partial C_f}{\partial Z} > 0$, that is, increased family size causes

an increase in food demand, and therefore $\dfrac{\partial R}{\partial Z} < 0$. If larger family size tends to

be associated with poverty, then this would also cause the poor to be less commercialized.

So the basic household model already implies a negative relationship between poverty and extent of commercialization, though it does not suggest that the poor will not respond to price incentives by increasing their commercial sales. However, because of the separability property, this model does _not_ suggest that production patterns will be influenced by poverty or food security concerns.

Introducing Quotas into the Model

The Chinese government still partially controls marketing of foodgrains by imposing quotas, or compulsory contracts, for sale to the government at administered prices. It simultaneously resells foodgrains to grain deficit or cash crop-growing households. The resale price is usually higher than quota or contract price due to transportation cost. Does this partially-administered pricing system change conclusions drawn from the basic model?

These interventions will change the budget constraint as follows:

(2.1) $Q_f P_q + P_f(F_f - Q_f - (C_f - R_r)) + E + F_c P_c = P_r R_r + P_n C_n$

$F_f - Q_f - C_f + R_r > 0$ => net sale

$F_f - Q_f - C_f + R_r < 0$ => net purchase

where Q_f quota sales

P_q quota price at the farmgate

R_r resale of food

P_r resale price

and others as before.

The quota is fixed by government and is exogenous to household decision making, so:

(2.6) $Q_f = q$ {Quota constraint}

As resale grain is usually priced at less than the market price, government limits the quantity which a household can buy to the difference between its food "surplus" (production minus quota sales) and an estimate of need based on family composition. This can be expressed as:

(2.7) $0 \le R_r \le (F_f - Q_f) - T(Z)$ {Resale constraint}

where $T(Z)$ is a "ration formula." Note that households which are left too little grain because of (i) low production, (ii) high quotas, or (iii) specialization in cash crops, all could be entitled to purchase resale grain.

Since the resale price is the quota procurement price plus the transport cost from supplying to purchasing areas, the resale price will vary with the distance the grain is transported. This can be reflected in models with a spatial dimension by making $P_r = P_q + t(d)$, where the transport cost t is a function of distance d from supplying to purchasing areas, and substituting in the equations above (see also similar analysis below applied to market prices).

The Lagrangian equation is follows:

$$(2.8) \quad \mathcal{L} = U(C_f, C_n, Z) + \lambda(Q_f P_q + P_f(F_f - Q_f - (C_f - R_r))) + E + F_c P_c - P_r R_r - P_n C_n)$$
$$+ \mu[F(F_f, L_f, A_f)] + \phi[G(F_c, \bar{L}-L_f, \bar{A}-A_f)] + \theta[R_r - (F_f - Q_f) + T(Z)]$$

The first- and second-order conditions are again left to the Annex. The Hessian remains block diagonal, so the separability property still holds if there is an internal solution. This differs from Sicular's (1986) conclusion based on a similar but not identical model of the impact of fixed quotas. The key difference is that our model has assumed that farmers may sell on the free market grain production in excess of quota sales, and may purchase grain from the free market to supplement own-production or purchases at official resale prices. Sicular, however, assumes no market sales or purchases -- only quota sales and consumption from own-production. Thus our product market is complete, whereas Sicular's is incomplete. Her model was an appropriate description of the Chinese collective farming system during the period prior to the economic reform, when free markets in grain were prohibited. Our model is equally appropriate for recent years, following decollectivization and the restoration of free markets, and despite the retention of grain sales quotas. One could say, then, that separability in consumption and production decision-making may result from the economic reforms.

However, corner solutions may also occur -- for example, a farmer may be forced by the quota to produce more grain than free market prices would dictate. Farmers with comparative advantage in cash crops (or responding to relatively high cash crop prices) might produce no more of food crops than the quota. The result is allocative inefficiency and reduced incomes, though separability still holds. Compared to a situation where only free marketing exists (the basic model), a larger proportion of farmers will be operating with corner solutions.

From the Hessian matrix, equation (2.9) in the Annex, for farmers at internal solutions, food consumption responds negatively to an increase in the food sales quota through the profit effect:

$$(2.11) \qquad \frac{\partial C_f}{\partial Q_f} = (P_q - P_f)\frac{\partial C_f}{\partial E}$$

where $P_q - P_f < 0$ is the effect of increased quota on farm incomes. The marketed surplus of food (quota plus free market sales) will increase due entirely to decreased consumption (total production will be unaffected, as free market prices determine the optimum production level). The commercial rate will also increase with higher quota (so long as only market prices are used in computing value of sales, as in the denominator of equation 1.13).

Neither the quota price nor the resale price appears in the Hessian except in the budget constraint, because an internal solution implies that production of food exceeds the quota and consumption exceeds the resale amount, so substitution effects in both production and consumption are influenced by free market prices only. However, all prices received enter the determination of farm profits, so the profit effect will be sensitive to quota as well as other prices. If all prices increase by the same proportion, the profit effect will be larger than it would be if only market (or non-quota) prices increase. Since the profit effect in response to increased prices tends to increase consumption, the increase in consumption will be smaller (increase in market surplus larger) if quota prices are kept constant when other prices increase. In another words, the introduction of a fixed quota and maintenance of an unchanging quota price would increase the marketed surplus response to crop price increases compared to a unified market price system. To a government particularly concerned about increasing market surpluses, the usefulness of the quota system is quite apparent.

Introducing Labor Market and Labor-Leisure Choice

In rural China, although land is leased to individual farm households by the state, a true land market still has not formed. Only in a few highly-developed areas, farmers who are engaged in nonfarming businesses rent their land to farmers migrating from underdeveloped areas. Within a village, farmers farm the land contracted to them, and there is no legal provision for land rental (although land can be "returned" to the collective and allocated to someone else, and some compensation may be made). However, there is definitely a wage-labor market for rural labor, for both non-farm and farm activities. If we introduce a labor market, but continue to treat land as a fixed input, does it change our results from the basic model?

Labor hired in and out at market wage rates will change the budget constraint as follows (the labor endowment constraint, as in equation 1.4, is eliminated; and the budget constraint now represents "full income", including the value of leisure):

(3.1) $P_f(F_f - C_f) + F_c P_c + w(T - C_l - L_f - L_c)$

$= P_n C_n$ {Budget constraint}

where

$T - C_l - L_f - L_c > 0$ labor hired out

$T - C_l - L_f - L_c < 0$ labor hired in

and T = time endowment (of labor), C_l = consumption of leisure, and w = market wage rate. L_f and L_c now include both hired and family labor.

Leisure is a consumable, and should be an argument in the utility function, i.e., $U(C_f, C_n, C_l)$.   In the basic model, with fixed labor and no labor market, we avoided introducing leisure as a consumable in order to preserve separability and simplify the analysis of comparative statics. We can now afford to introduce leisure **because the introduction of a labor market will preserve the separability property**.

The Lagrangian equation is:

(3.2) $\mathscr{L} = U(C_f, C_n, C_l) + \lambda[P_f(F_f - C_f) + F_c P_c + w(T - C_l - L_f - L_c) - P_n C_n] +$

$\mu[F(F_f, L_f, A_f)] + \phi[G(F_c, L_c, \bar{A} - A_f]$

The modified first- and second-order conditions are given in the Annex. The first point to note is that the Hessian remains block diagonal, i.e., separability still holds. As the first order conditions indicate, the fundamental optimization conditions of

$$(3.5) \quad \frac{p_c \, G_L}{G_c} = \frac{p_f \, F_L}{F_F} = w \; , \text{where} \quad \frac{G_L}{G_c} \quad \text{and} \quad \frac{F_L}{F_F} \quad \text{are the marginal productivities}$$

of labor in cash and food cropping respectively. These equations do not include consumption of food, non-food or leisure as endogenous variables. That is, total labor and amounts used for each crop are determined by wage rates, marginal productivities, and prices of each crop alone.

From the Annex, the right-hand-side expression of the fourth equation in (3.3), it is apparent that equations (1.9-1.11) still hold. **Price response is the same in a model with no labor market but also no demand for leisure, as in a model with labor-leisure choice but also a labor market with exogenous wage.** Changes in wages have an effect on the consumption of leisure described by:

$$(3.6) \quad \frac{\partial C_l}{\partial w} = \frac{\partial C_l}{\partial w}\Big|_U + (T - C_l - L_f - L_c)\frac{\partial C_l}{\partial Y}$$

As in equation (1.9), the result is unambiguous only if the household is a net hirer of labor, in which case the family labor supply curve is positively sloped; otherwise a backward-bending labor supply curve cannot be ruled out.

Finally, it is apparent that the signs of **the relationship between commercialization and poverty (with land endowment as proxy for wealth, i.e., equation 1.14) and commercialization and food security are not affected**, as the model is still separable.

Introducing Transport Cost

The basic model assumed that sales and purchase prices are homogeneous, but this is not realistic. Farmers sell at farmgate prices at one season, buy at retail prices at another season. There is likely to be a wedge between buying and selling prices. How does this affect our conclusions?

Transport cost is largely a function of distance between farm and marketplace. If we take the price <u>at the market</u> to be P_f, then the farmgate price of food sold by the farmer will be $P_f - t$, and the farmgate price for food purchased by the farmer will be $P_f + t$, where t can vary with distance between farm and market (the same technically applies to cash crops, but since, by assumption, they are not purchased by the farmer, we treat P_c as a farmgate price). This differential between selling and purchase prices for the same item at the farmgate may be important in explaining self-sufficiency orientation. The budget constraint becomes:

$$(4.1) \quad Q_f P_q + P^*(F_f - Q_f - (C_f - R_r)) + F_c P_c + w(\bar{L} - L_f - L_c)$$

$$= P_r R_r + P_n C_n + r(\bar{A} - A_f - A_c) \quad \{\text{Budget constraint}\}$$

where $P^* = P_f + t$ if $F_f - Q_f - C_f + R_r < 0$ (net purchaser of food)

and $\quad P^* = P_f - t$ if $F_f - Q_f - C_f + R_r > 0$ (net seller of food)

P* is an implicit price and replaces P_f in the model, thus the interior solution (first-order and second-order conditions) is nominally unchanged. However, in fact the price "wedge" can cause significant differences in the behaviour of net sellers, net purchases, and self-sufficient producers.

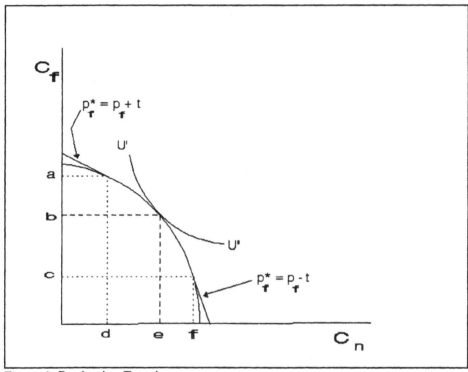

Figure 9. Production Frontier

Consider Figure 9, where the production optimization conditions have been "collapsed" to show a single "production frontier" (given certain amounts of fixed and variable inputs); and units of production of the cash crop have been converted into purchasable units of the non-food consumer good, at exogenous price ratio p_c/p_a: in maximizing utility (ignoring leisure as an argument), the farmer may end up with an indifference curve tangent to (a) the budget line determined by p^* = p_f + t, in which case he produces at **ad** and becomes a net purchaser of food; or (b) to the budget line p^* = p_f - t, in which he produces at **cf** and becomes a net seller; or (c) somewhere in between, in which case he both produces and consumes **be** and is self-sufficient. The wider the price wedge *t*, the larger is the range of conditions under which the farmer will choose self-sufficiency. Moreover, the self-sufficient farmer does <u>not</u> respond to modest changes in p_f with changes in either production or consumption -- rather, he ignores market prices and looks only at the marginal rates of transformation in production and of substitution in the utility function. Only radical changes in prices will induce a market involvement. On the other hand, farmers who become deficit or surplus food producers respond normally to small price changes. (Compare SSS, 1986, pp. 53-54, which discuss a price wedge in the labor market. The slope of the tangent of U'U" in Figure 9 to the production frontier determines the "virtual" or shadow price they refer to).

For the deficit producer, the virtual price determining <u>both</u> consumption and production patterns is the higher price P_f + t, whereas for the surplus producer it is P_f - t; hence the deficit farmer will tend to be <u>more</u> specialized in food crop production while consuming relatively less food than the surplus producer, <u>ceteris</u> <u>paribus</u>.

Introducing Risk and Risk Aversion

Adapting Finkelshtain and Chalfant's and Fafchamps' models to our notation, the model assumes that producers maximize the expected value of a utility function defined over two commodities -- a self-consumed crop ("food", or C_f) and an "aggregate market good" (C_a) -- while producing the former (F_f), here food production per hectare) and a cash crop (F_c):

(5.1) $\max E\{U(C_f, C_a, Z)\}$, $U' > 0$, $U'' < 0$ on C_f and C_a

subject to an income constraint,

$$p_f C_f + p_a C_a <= y(A) = p_f F_f A_f + p_c F_c A_c = \pi_f A_f + \pi_c A_c$$

where $y(A)$ = income resulting from production using the single fixed factor, land (A); π_f and π_c are net revenues per hectare, and other terms are defined as previously; except that p_f, p_c, F_f, and F_c are all random variables, so $Y(A)$ is a random variable. (Finkelshtain and Chalfant include leisure in the utility function with an opportunity cost equal to the wage rate; following Fafchamps, I omit this in order to focus on the choice between crops only.)

Since production decisions are made at time $t=0$ and consumption decisions at $t=1$, when the "outcomes" (actual production and prices) are known, hence not random variables, it is mathematically useful to define the "variable indirect utility function" (Epstein, 1975) as the function defining the maximum utility the family can obtain given first-period outcomes (prices, production levels, and resulting revenues):

(5.2) $V[y(A), p_f, p_a] \equiv \max \{U(C_f, C_a, Z) \mid p_f C_f + p_a C_a <= y(A)$

where $y(A) \geq 0$, and p_f, $p_a > 0$,

Thus (5.1) may be restated in terms of the variable indirect utility function in (5.2) as:

(5.3) max $E\{V[Y(A), p_f, p_n, A_f, A_c]\}$

subject to $y(A) = \pi_f A_f + \pi_c A_c$,

where $A_f + A_c = \bar{A}$ (land) with respect to the decision variables A_f and A_c, and

A_f, $A_c \geq 0$.

This formulation leaves Y and vector p as random variables. However, Epstein, Finkelshtain and Chalfant, and Fafchamps all use slightly simpler variations on this model, and all their derived implications for decision-making under risk aversion should apply. Fafchamps' approach, which is based on a Taylor series expansion of the first-order conditions for maximization of (5.3) and a manipulation of terms into parameters with intuitive appeal (expenditure shares, income elasticities, relative risk aversion, ratio of expected returns, coefficient of variation of prices and revenues, and the correlation between prices and revenues), provides the most useful results far testing with panel data, and will be followed here (even though, strictly speaking, the Taylor series expansion is valid only for small risks).

The interior optimal solution is from first order conditions:

$$\frac{\partial E[V]}{\partial A_f} = E[V_y \pi_f] = 0$$

$$\frac{\partial E[V]}{\partial A_c} = E[V_y \pi_c] = 0 \quad \text{or}$$

(5.4) $E[V_y(\pi_f - \pi_c)] = 0$

The producer is assumed income risk averse, that is $V_{yy}(y, p_i) < 0$ for all p and y, which is sufficient to ensure that the second-order condition for interior solution is met.

V_y can be approximated using a Taylor series expansion around average prices $\bar{P}_f$ and $\bar{P}_c$ and income $\bar{Y}$:

(5.5) $V_y \approx \bar{V}_y + \sum_{k=1}^{M} \bar{V}_{yp_i}(P_k - \bar{P}_k) + \bar{V}_{yy}(Y - \bar{Y})$ where $\bar{V}_y$ is the evaluation of V_y at

mean income and prices, and k here represents only two commodities, food and non-food.

The further manipulations of (5.5) are left to the Annex, where the additional equations (5.6) and (5.7) are derived. These allow us to solve for the optimal proportion of acreage in the food crop f:

(5.8) $A_f^* \approx \dfrac{-(P+Q)-\psi S}{(m-1)(P+Q)+\psi T}$

where $T = CV_{\pi_c}^2 + m_f^2\, CV_{\pi_f}^2 + (1-m_f)^2 - 2m_f\, \rho_{\pi_c\pi_f} CV_{\pi_c} CV_{\pi_f}$

$S = m\rho_{\pi_c\pi_f} CV_{\pi_c} CV_{\pi_f} - CV_{\pi_c}^2 + m_f - 1$

The optimal crop portfolio is a function of expenditure share of food s_k, income elasticity η_f, coefficient of relative risk aversion ψ, coefficients of correlation between price and revenue $\rho_{\pi p}$, and coefficients of variation of price and revenue.

To simplify notation, assume that crop revenues are independent of the price of non-produced consumption goods (eliminating half of term Q in 5.7) and use A_f in place of part of the remainder of Q:

$$
\begin{aligned}
Q &= CV_{p_f}(\rho_{\pi_c P_f} CV_{\pi_c} - m\rho_{\pi_r P_f} CV_{\pi_r}) s_f(\eta_f - \psi) \\
&= B_f s_f(\eta_f - \psi) \\
\text{where } B_f &= \frac{1}{E(p_f)E(\pi_c)}[\sigma_{\pi_c P_f} - \sigma_{\pi_r P_f}]
\end{aligned}
$$

(5.9)

Rewriting the first order condition (5.8) as $g(A^*)$ and deriving the second order condition (H),

$$
g(A^*_f) = A^*_f((m-1)(P+Q)+\psi T) + (P+Q)+\psi s = 0
$$

(5.10)

$$
\text{and } H = \frac{\partial g}{\partial A^*_f} = ((m-1)(P+Q)+\psi T) < 0 \qquad \text{for an interior solution to}
$$

hold. Taking derivatives of A^* with respect to s_f, we can explore how the optimal food crop proportion would vary with the budget share of food:

(5.11)

$$
\frac{\partial A^*_f}{\partial s_f} \approx \frac{-B_f(\eta_f-\psi)[1+A^*_f(m-1)]}{H}
$$

Since $H < 0$, $m > 0$, and $A^* \leq 1$, the sign of (5.11) is the same as that of $B_f(\eta_f-\psi)$.

Four possibilities determine the sign of dA^*/ds_f:

Positive	Negative
$B_f > 0$ $\eta_f - \psi > 0$	$B_f > 0$ $\eta_f - \psi < 0$
$B_f < 0$ $\eta_f - \psi < 0$	$B_f < 0$ $\eta_f - \psi > 0$

Usually, the income elasticity of food crop is less than one, while income relative risk aversion is greater than one (Newbery and Stiglitz, 1981; Turnovsky, Shalit, and Schmitz, 1980), so the expression $\eta_f - \psi$ can be expected to be negative. The sign of B_f, on the other hand, depends on whether $cov\ (\pi_f, p_f)$ is greater than or less than $cov\ (\pi_c, p_f)$. Fafchamps argues that "generally the covariance between the price of one crop and the revenue of the other is smaller than the covariance between price and revenue of the same crop". This does not seem to be true even if price is the only source of covariance, but is certainly not obvious if production risk is also a major source of covariance. Signing and evaluating the size of these two covariances requires further recourse to the empirical characteristics of staple food crop production.

First, it is likely that the market for staple food is more localized than the market for the cash crop (most staple food is consumed locally, but most cash crops are processed outside of the rural areas and enter into the national or even international economy, so that prices are insensitive to local crop conditions except in major cash-crop production areas). Second, production risk among locally-produced crops is likely to be positively intercorrelated (affected similarly by common environmental conditions). For these reasons, the covariance between price and yield of staple food is almost certainly negative (local market assumption); between yields of staple food and cash crops positive (shared production risk); and between the price of the cash crop and either price or yield of staple food crop a zero covariance can be expected (national cash crop market). Together, these imply that the covariance between the price of staple food and the revenues from the cash crop cov (π_c, p_f) would be negative.

On the other hand, the sign and magnitude of cov (π_f, p_f) depends mainly on the price elasticity of demand. For staple foods, demand is likely to be price inelastic, and in this case revenue decreases when quantity increases (and price falls). That is, if P is the demand curve and R = Pq, then

$$\frac{\partial R}{\partial q} = P(1 - \frac{1}{\zeta}) < 0, \text{ where } \zeta = - \frac{P}{q}\frac{\partial q}{\partial p} < 1 . \text{ Thus } cov \ (\pi_f, p_f) > 0, \text{ and}$$

$$A_f \ (\eta_f - \psi) = [cov(\pi_c p_f) - cov(\pi_p p_f)](\eta_f - \psi) > 0 . \text{ We conclude, with Fafchamps,}$$

that the "risk-averse farmer whose share of food in total expenditure is large will produce proportionally more food than a similarly risk-averse farmer whose share of food in total expenditure is small. Only farmers with a low share of food in total expenditures will devote a significant amount of resources to cash crop production." This result depends, however, on the characteristics of the pair of crops chosen, including the localization of the market for staple foods and the integration of the market for cash crops.

Considering also the effect of higher income elasticity of demand for food on staple food crop proportion,L, the relationship similar to (5.9) is easily derived, and we find

$$dL_i/d\eta_i < 0 \text{ when } cov(\pi_i, p_i) > cov(\pi_j, p_i)$$

or the farmers with higher income elasticities of demand for food will reduce production of food crop. Normally, growing a consumption crop (here, food), the revenues of which are correlated with prices, provides insurance against price risk in consumption. The desire for such insurance is not the same on the part of every consumer, but is a reflection of the convexity of the indirect utility function in p_f. As Turnovsky, Shalit and Shmitz (1980), indicate, the indirect utility function is generally only quasi-convex in prices, though convex in income; and thus aversion to income risk does not necessarily imply aversion to price risk for all commodities. Turnovsky, Shalit and Shmitz further show that, for the case of a pure consumer (income is exogenous):

$$(5.12) \quad \sigma = \frac{-\partial^2 V/\partial p_f^2 \cdot p_f}{\partial V/\partial p_f} = s_f(\eta_f - \psi) - \zeta_f \text{ , where } \sigma \text{ is a measure of relative risk}$$

aversion with respect to price risk, similar to ρ.

Thus σ decreases (becomes less negative) with higher income elasticity of demand, as well as higher price elasticity and budget share, but increases with increased relative income risk aversion. Because relative price risk aversion decreases with higher income elasticities, the insurance against price risk offered by cultivating the crop (food) is less valued and so a smaller proportion of area is devoted to the crop. (While this may seem counterintuitive, as poor farmers have higher income elasticity of demand for food and typically are thought more likely to grow a higher proportion of the food crop, it should be recognized that poor farmers probably have higher income risk aversion, which has an opposite effect on σ.)

Returning to our producer-consumer, the effect of income risk aversion, $dL^*/d\psi$ is the same sign as[12] $\quad -B_f s_f + 1 - m + \dfrac{A \cdot T + S}{1 + A \cdot (m-1)}$, which combines

two effects, the consumption effect in $A_f s_f$ (considered also by Turnovsky, Shalit and Shmitz), and a risky portfolio (or diversification) effect

---

[12] These terms differ from Fafchamps' due to correction of sign errors in the derivation and elimination of his extra term $B_1 S_1$, which should be zero by his own assumption of independence between crop revenues and the price of non-produced consumption goods. The errors in Fafchamps' expression for the "portfolio effect" can be demonstrated by examining what happens to this term in the case of zero risk (it should, but does not, become zero).

$$1-m+\frac{A^{*}T + S}{1+A^{*}(m-1)} = -\frac{cov(y,\ \pi_f - \pi_c)}{\bar{y}E[\pi_c]}$$ As the consumption effect is positive, the

more risk-averse farmers will tend to grow more staple food (consumption good) to provide more insurance against price risk, but this may be qualified or accentuated by the desire to diversify crops as a protection against income risk (depending on the sign of a covariance term which is obscure).

Conclusions. Summing up the effects of several key variables on the crop portfolio, we find that the relative importance of the food crop depends mainly on consumption share and risk aversion, as well as risk in both prices and production. Other things being equal, one would expect poor farmers, with high risk aversion, high budget share in food, and price inelastic demand, to grow a relatively higher proportion of staple food on their farm areas than wealthy farmers, whose budget share in food is smaller and risk aversion lower. These effects, of course, are in addition to such influences on comparative advantage as the expected prices, yields, and variations in yields of the two crops.

The relationship between poverty and food security, in the context of this model, can be viewed as equivalent to the relationship between expected income $\bar{y}$ and the proportion of acreage in the staple food crop. If we simplify by assuming relative risk aversion and the income elasticity of demand for food to be invariant with respect to expected income (not assumptions likely to apply to the poorest farmers), as Fafchamps shows, the relationship is unambiguous in sign:

$$\frac{\partial A^*}{\partial \bar{y}} >(<) \; 0 \; as \; \frac{B_f \, s_f \, (\eta_f - 1)(\eta_f - \psi)}{\bar{y}} >(<) \; 0 \; and, \; on \; the \; assumptions \; given$$

above, the sign must be negative. That is, poorer farmers will tend to grow a higher proportion of staple food crops.

Relaxing Fafchamp's simplifying assumptions in order to look at the case of the poorest farmers in poor countries, it is likely that relative risk aversion increases with decreased expected income (indeed, becoming infinite at a true "subsistence level")(Newbery and Stiglitz. 1981). Also, the income elasticity of demand for staple foods most likely decreases with increased expected income, especially at higher income levels. If relative risk aversion and income elasticity of demand both change with income levels, the term $+ B_f s_f \left(\frac{\partial \eta_f}{\partial \bar{y}} - \frac{\partial \psi}{\partial \bar{y}}\right)$ must be added to the expression the sign of which we are evaluating. This sign may seem ambiguous, but at levels of income near subsistence, the absolute magnitude of $\frac{\partial \psi}{\partial \bar{y}}$ is likely to be much greater than $\frac{\partial \eta_f}{\partial \bar{y}}$. Thus relaxing Fafchamp's assumptions should strengthen the conclusion of the previous paragraph.

The extent of <u>commercialization</u> of the farmer is not explicitly represented in this model. However, it is apparent that the rate of commercialization (cash sales divided by total production value) will tend to vary inversely with A_f, the proportion of crop area in food (as at least part of the food is not sold, whereas all of the cash crop is sold). As seen above, both increased poverty and increased risk aversion should be associated with increased A_f (decreased A_c), hence decreased commercialization rates. Also higher s_f (reflecting food security concerns) was shown to be associated with increased A_f or a lesser degree of cash cropping. All of these relationships are fundamentally due to the insurance which growing of self-consumed crops gives against price risk in consumption. If there were no price variations, these relationships would not exist -- relative production risks alone would affect the choice between food and cash crops, and this would be unpredictable without explicit knowledge of the production environment and technologies.

C. Testable Hypotheses

The theoretical models above give an insight into the relationships among poverty, food security and commercialization. Although statistical data to fully estimate these models are absent, nevertheless each of the models developed implies the following hypotheses which can be tested through an econometric model by employing household data. Thus we would be able to answer the questions raised in the beginning of this thesis, of **(1) whether food insecurity is still a major**

characteristic of the poor, and (2) whether commercialization is positively correlated with income or food security (or whether the poor concentrate on food production and are less commercialized due to concern for food security), which can be seen from the following chart:

	Poverty	Food Insecurity	Commercialization
Poverty		+	-
Food Insecurity	+		-
Commercialization	-	-	

The first question may be examined by grouping households according to different levels of poverty (defined alternatively as the poor in income and as residents of poor counties) and food security (food self-sufficiency and consumption adequacy), and then testing for significant differences in food security between the poor and non-poor.

The second question requires that we examine the responsiveness of marketed surplus to price for different groups. However, the response of marketed surplus depends on a combination of demand, supply and labor supply of the households and some exogenous factors (e.g., quota procurement, transport cost, and risk in production and prices) as well. Therefore, we will test the responsiveness of marketed surplus as well as that of production and consumption to the variation of prices and income through a full household model. As data on labor and wage rate is lacking, the response of labor supply must be omitted.

On the production side, the hypothesis is:

(1) The response of farm production, both of grain growers and cash crop growers, to own-price variation is expected to be positive, and in response to cross-price variation, negative, as described in conventional microeconomics theory.

On the consumption side, the significance of the profit effect will be tested:

(2) The response of farm consumption of food to increased price of food is ambiguous when the profit effect is considered, i.e.,

$$\frac{\partial C_f}{\partial p_f} = \frac{\partial C_f}{\partial p_f}\bigg|_U + \frac{\partial C_f}{\partial p_f}\frac{\partial p_f}{\partial \pi} \lessgtr 0 .$$

The strength of the profit effect increases with increased share of food in production revenue, and with increased income elasticity of demand. Since the poor, whose budget share of food is large, are likely to have higher income elasticities of demand than the rich, the poor will be more likely to have small or positive price elasticities of consumption, and are likely to be more specialized in food production than richer farmers, based on the conclusions from the previous household models.

(3)   The consumption of all goods, food or non-food, should respond
        positively to variation of cash crop price through the profit effect, i.e.,

$$\frac{\partial C_i}{\partial p_c} = \frac{\partial C_i}{\partial p_c}\bigg|_U + \frac{\partial C_i}{\partial p_c}\frac{\partial p_c}{\partial Y}\frac{\partial Y}{\partial \pi} > 0 \ .$$

        Combining supply and demand responses, the hypotheses for marketed
surplus are follows:

(4)   The market surplus for food depends on a combination of the effects of
        production and consumption, some of which are ambiguous or opposite
        in sign, so it is difficult to predict how marketed surplus will vary with
        price or other variables. Net food purchasers are an exception, for which
        the market surplus price elasticity should be positive, that is, an increase
        in food price will lead to decreased purchases (Strauss, 1986). Overall,
        the models imply that commercialization (but not necessarily that of food
        production) will increase with increased wealth and food security.

(5)   The existence of quota procurement and quota prices does not change
        the above conclusions for farmers with internal solutions; and therefore
        quota prices should not be included in estimation of a agricultural
        household models based on such solutions. However, quota procurement
        should increase the frequency of corner solutions, where choice of crop
        areas is not consistent with relative prices. The presence of <u>corner</u>
        <u>solutions</u> can be tested by examining the <u>frequency</u> with which farmers

produce no more than the sum of quotas and consumption requirements, i.e., are not net sellers or buyers of grain at market prices. Also, if a large proportion of the sample is at such corner solutions, one would not expect to find large or statistically significant price elasticities of total supply.

(6)   The response of marketed surplus to increased transportation cost should be negative, and the existence of price wedges between farm sales and purchase prices might also cause a higher proportion of corner solutions. However, without survey data on transportation cost or distance to market places, this is not easily tested; and such data is not commonly collected in household surveys.

Most farmers in developing countries are risk-averse (Hammer, 1986). However, it is difficult to measure risk attitudes. It is, therefore, equally hard to directly test the response of production, consumption and marketed surplus to risk aversion because we cannot measure utility functions reliably. It is, thus, necessary to rely on indirect forms of inference. The appeal of Fafchamps' paper is that assumptions about risk and risk aversion are used to derive relations between proportions of crop area in food crops and variations in the budget share of food, income elasticity of demand for food, relative risk aversion measure, coefficient of variation of price and revenue (as risk measures), and correlations between price and revenue. Under reasonable (but not necessarily valid) assumptions, Fafchamps shows that a risk-averse farmer whose budget share of food in total expenditure is large will be more specialized (or allocate most land on) in the food crop than a farmer whose budget share is smaller; or, only farmers whose food budget share is small will devote more resources to cash crops. The testable hypothesis for risk factor, therefore, is:

(7) poverty should be associated with subsistence orientation and wealth with commercialization and specialization in cash crops, since poor farmers probably have higher risk aversion, higher budget share in food, and price inelastic demand for food -- if there is sufficient price risk. Although the causes cannot be firmly identified without knowing the magnitudes of risks or degree of risk aversion, even a basic model, free of risk or risk aversion, suggests that commercialization rate and income levels would be correlated as seen above.

V. STATISTICAL AND ECONOMETRIC ANALYSIS

The objective of this section is to test the hypotheses made in previous section using the 1988 10,000 rural household CASS-UCR data set. The approach is to econometrically estimate a nearly complete household decision-making model focused on consumption and production decisions for foods, and then employ it to examine marketing and market purchase behaviour.

The sample will be grouped in various ways during estimation to highlight (1) differences across income groups, (2) between residents of poverty areas and residents of other areas, and (3) between food secure and insecure households. Commercialization is treated both as an endogenous outcome of decisions on production, consumption and marketing (a commercial rate) and as an inferred behavioral tendency (willingness to increase market sales in response to price increases). The model to be estimated will be the basic household model introduced in the previous section. The equation form hypothesized for supply is the Constant Elasticity of Transformation-Cobb Douglas (CET-CD), and for demand, the Quadratic Expenditure System (QES) (both were introduced in II-C-2 above). Some simplification of the models are made due to limitations of our data set and difficulties encountered in econometric estimation. We also take account of the conclusions drawn from variations on the basic model in our analysis of the data.

A. **Specification of the Model**

Basic Assumptions. The basic household model in Section II has a general solution for separate demand and supply equations (derivable from the Hessian matrix equation (1.8) in the Annex I). However, some special assumption have to be made due to incomplete data. As information on labor and the labor market is entirely absent, the model must ignore the labor-leisure choice (as we did in our basic model). Land, fixed capital, and fertilizer are the major production inputs represented. Of these, the first two can reasonably be assumed fixed in the short run in China, leaving the fertilizer as the only variable production input. Household size is available as a proxy for labor, but its inclusion in the model makes sense only if it is also considered a fixed input -- that is, we must assume no hired labor and make full use of family labor on-farm.

Household consumption in the estimation model should normally include all commodities and services. However, consumption data are available only on three aggregate goods, i.e., staple food (various grains and tubers), nonstaple food (livestock products, vegetables, and edible oil), and other food (tea, sugar, fruit, and liquid), and not on non-food commodities or services. Except for staple food, these aggregate categories are not found on the production side, where only production of individual products is available. This makes it difficult to match supply and demand equations. Worse, non-staple food is a troublesome aggregate, composed of high value meat (which only indirectly, through feed production, uses the same inputs as crops) and low value vegetables and oilseeds. It is far easier to conceive of non-staple foods as a meaningful consumption category than as a production category.

Demand Side. A Quadratic Expenditure System (QES) is used to estimate the demand side of the model (Section II C 2). Use of the QES avoids some limitations of the LLES, such as imposing unitary elasticities of expenditure with respect to full income, and the LES, such as the restriction of linear Engel curves. QES allows for a more flexible relationship between full income and commodity expenditure, and this is important because of the intention to look in detail at changes in parameters over different income groups.

Since QES is a model of a household rather than an individual, there is a need to incorporate household characteristics, such as household size or age distribution, which may affect utility. The method used is termed translation, which involves subtracting commodity-specific indices from arguments in the direct utility function, i.e. $U(X) = U(X_1-V_1, X_2-V_2, ...X_n-V_n)$, where V_i is a function of household characteristics. Since T (whether defined as total time available to the household or as leisure time available) is unknown, T may also be treated as a simple function of household characteristics (e.g., number of hours per person times household size) and replaced in the utility function. So including household characteristics in translation form and omitting T has the effect that the estimated translation coefficients will be a composite measuring the direct impact of these characteristics on the utility function as well as the indirect impact through total leisure time available.

In our estimation of this model, first, the data include the expenditure only on three aggregated food commodities (staple, non-staple, and other), so only three equations could be estimated and prices of non-food consumer goods and services had to be omitted. Lacking relevant commodities, the sums of α_k and δ_k also need not be unity. This causes specification error and bias in the included coefficients to the extent that included variables are correlated with excluded variables. Secondly, household size is the only household characteristic available in the data; other relevant characteristics which undoubtedly affect demand, such as age composition, were omitted, and again may cause the results to be biased. Third, consumption habits (or utility functions) may differ as among households in regions with different overall living standards (just as relative poverty standards may differ among such regions). To account for such differences, dummy variables D_j are used (also using the translation form) to specific (a) residence in one of five regions differing by both standard and cost of living (see Chapter II)[13]; (b) residence in mountainous, hilly, or plains areas.

Hence the model actually estimated, for i = staple food, non-staple food, and other food, was:

---

[13] Ranging from wealthiest to poorest, these are (1) Beijing, Tianjin, Shanghai; (2) Guangdong, Zhejiang, Jiangsu, Liaoning; (3) Hebei, Jilin, Heilongjiang, Fujian, Jiangxi, Shandong, Hubei, Hunan, Xinjiang; (4) Shansi, Anhui, Henan, Neimenggu, Qinghai, Ningxia, Sichuan, Guizhou, Yunnan, Guangxi; (5) Shaanxi, Gansu, Xizang. This differentiation comes from a Chinese study of poverty (RGCPA, 1990).

(V.1)
$$p_iX_i = p_if_i + \alpha_i (\pi + E - \sum_{k=1}^{3} p_k(c_k + \epsilon H + \sum_{j=1}^{6} r_jD_j))$$
$$-(\alpha_i - \delta_i) \prod_{k=1}^{3} p_k^{(-\delta_i)} (\pi + E - \sum_{k=1}^{3} p_k(c_k+\epsilon H + \sum_{j=1}^{6} r_jD_j))^2$$

where E = exogenous income,

p_k = prices of goods, k = 1,...,N - 1,

π = short-run net income

= value of all outputs less the value of variable inputs (excluding family labor)

H = Household size, and

D_j are the dummies.[14]

Production Side. On the production side, all input data are aggregated, not separated by product, while output data are separate. The CET-CD equation form (see Section II-C-2) is therefore adopted, in which a constant elasticity of transformation (CET) is used to specify outputs, while a Cobb-Douglas (CD) equation can be used to specify aggregated inputs. This in turn is used to derive supply functions for each output, with equations of the form:

$$Q_i = \beta_L^{\beta_L/1-\beta_L} d_i^{-1/(\rho-1)} p_i^{1/(\rho-1)} (\sum_k d_k^{-1/(\rho-1)} p_k^{\rho/(\rho-1)})^{(\rho\beta_L-1)/\rho(1-\beta_L)}$$
$$(A^{\beta_A} K^{\beta_K})^{1/(1-\beta_L)} w^{[-\beta_L/(1-\beta_L)]}$$

where p_i are product prices and d_i, ρ and β_L are parameters, and

---

[14] To prevent singularity, dummies for region (3) and mountainous areas are taken as base conditions.

Q_i = production of good i, i = 1, ..., M,

L = labor use (family plus hired),

A = total cultivated area,

K = capital flow, and

w = wage rate.

However, although in China labor in many areas may indeed be regarded as a variable input, optimized with respect to the wage rate, we have no data on wage rates, and only household size to serve as a proxy for (family) labor. Also, Chinese agriculture is input-intensive, and at least current inputs (fertilizer, etc.) must be considered variable rather than fixed. Mathematical derivation of an appropriate supply function from the CET-CD production function when more than one input is regarded as variable is intractable. Therefore, we are forced to take current inputs (with fertilizer as the proxy) as the only variable input and labor as a fixed input. Some efficiency may be lost through use of a proxy for labor and some bias could be introduced through omission of the wage rate as a parameter of the supply function.

Separability is assumed, which allows separate estimation of demand and supply side; however, error terms in demand functions for each commodity and supply functions for each commodity are not independent, and the demand and supply equations should be estimated as systems of simultaneous equations. On the supply side, however, the problem arises that almost all farming households grow staple food (though non-farm rural households may not); but not every household grows any or all cash crops (of a total of six major crops recorded: cotton, oilseeds, jute/hemp, sugarcane/sugarbeet, tobacco, and vegetables) or engages in every activity (animal raising, forestry, and fishery). This is due to natural suitability of crops to particular areas and various economic factors, such as high transportation cost, unprofitable price ratios, and so on. Thus the production data, the dependent variables, are truncated (equivalent to saying that many farmers are at corner solutions for particular products, choosing not to produce; or else are unable to produce due to unsuitable production environment).

Applying Tobit estimation procedures to resolve this truncated data, which Strauss used to solve a similar problem, would be ideal. However, we were unable to find computer software able to estimate more than two non-linear equations using a combimation of Tobit, nonlinear, and simultaneous equation estimation procedures. Lacking reliable production data for the aggregate commodities "non-staple foods" and "other foods", included in the demand equations, there was little reason to be interested in results for products other than staple foods. Also, as few farms produced more than two crops (usually grain and oilseed or some other crop), simultaneous equation estimation for a multiple product model would have excluded most of the observations. Therefore, we chose to use single-equation estimation methods to estimate only one supply equation -- for staple food -- although prices of eight products are included as explanatory variables.

Cultivated land consists of two types -- irrigated and non-irrigated land, $A = A_i + A_d$. If we suppose that the ratio of marginal productivity on irrigated land to that of non-irrigated land equals a constant ß, a proper index combining the two types of land would be $I = A_d + ßA_i = A[1 + (ß-1)IA]$, where IA is percentage of

irrigated land (A_i/A). This linear form can directly enter the CD production function

in place of A. Alternatively, if we expect $1 < ß < 2$, we may replace the linear form

with an exponential form, $e^{ßIA}$, as an approximation for greater convenience in

estimation (Wiens, 1982). If the estimated elasticity coefficient on land is $ß_a^*$, then

an estimate of $ß$ can be derived as $\quad ß^* = 1 + \dfrac{ß_i^*}{ß_a^*} e^{\frac{ß_i^*}{ß_a^*}\bar{IA}}$, where $\bar{IA}$ is the sample

mean and the other coefficients are as estimated.

The same regional dummies used in demand function are used in the

supply function, in this case to reflect differences in production patterns and

productivity levels among different areas. These dummies are entered in exponential

(i.e., linear in logs) form in the supply function.

Prices are the most important factors in the model. *In both the supply and

demand side*, actual prices received or paid by the households are at least partly

endogenous (because prices vary over the year, and also vary with quality of product,

and these are choices made by the producer). To avoid problems which endogenous

right-hand-side variables would present for estimation, an average of market prices

for each county was taken to reflect the expected price faced by each producer.

(Strauss, 1986. This also provided appropriate price data for households which did not purchase or sell a particular commodity, even though they could have done so.)

The supply equation as shown in Section II-C-2 contains an additive term embedded within an otherwise log-linear equation. Estimation using iterative nonlinear methods did not result in convergence, due partly to singularity. As an alternative to use of non-linear estimation procedures, the summation term in prices taken to an exponent can also be approximated as a Taylor series expansion in the logs of prices (Bridge, 1971). In case that the elasticity of transformation among products is unity, the higher order terms entirely vanish. Even if the elasticity differs from unity, the first-order term in logs of prices can be regarded as an approximation to the summation term. Therefore, the equation was modified to one linear in logs (including logs of prices). Although some prices were zero, these were replaced with small positive values to prevent estimation from breaking down. Using a log linear function, however, causes a problem due to the assumption of constant price elasticities, whereas an objective is to test for variation in price elasticities across different groups. The easiest solution to this problem is to estimate separate supply functions for each income group (quintile) and other groups (poor areas vs non-poor areas, and food secure and food insecure groups), as discussed below.

Hence, the (single) supply equation actually estimated, for staple food, was (in log-linear form):

$$\text{ln } pdn = \beta + \sum_{i=1}^{8} \delta_i \text{ ln } p_i + \beta_1 \text{ln } A + \beta_2 \text{ln } K + \beta_3 I_A$$

(V.2)

$$+ \beta_4 \text{ ln } p_z + \beta_5 \text{ ln } H + \sum_{j=1}^{6} r_j D_j$$

where p_i are prices of seven crops plus pork, A is land, I_A is percentage of irrigated land, K is capital, H is household size, p_z is price of fertilizer, and D_j are regional/area dummies. Most coefficients are composites, as implied by Strauss' supply equation above.

Feed Demand. To derive marketed supply from production of staple food, one needs to know feed demand as well as human consumption, so a feed demand equation was estimated (without doing a full profit maximization model for livestock raising and feed use, for which some necessary parameters are missing from the data). There is a largely technical relationship between livestock product offtake (meat, eggs, etc.) and feed required, which can be reflected in the equation. Also a relation to prices should be included, as the ratio of meat to feed prices determines animal raising goals, which in turn determines feed requirements. The livestock products accounted for in the model are pork, hog, poultry, eggs, and large (draft) animals. Since pig raising is the predominant form of animal husbandry in China, the price of pork was used as the price of meat. The price ratio, therefore, is that of pork to staple food (i.e., grain). The equation used was quadratic in all variables, to approximate any non-linearities in the underlying feed demand function. The

equation was: $F = \gamma + \sum_{k=1}^{5} \alpha_k Z_k + \sum_{k=1}^{5} \beta_k Z_k^2 + \rho(\frac{P_p}{P_s})$

where F is feed, Z_t are livestock products, and P_p/P_g is the price ratio of pork to grain, and the remaining terms are parameters to be estimated.

B. Data Set

The data set used for econometric estimation was not collected specifically for this purpose, but rather its household survey data were collected under the project "Income Distribution in China", for a sample of about 10,258 rural households in 1988. The sample was drawn as a stratified subsample by income from the 67,186 household sample used in the SSB annual survey of rural income and consumption (Khan et al., 1992). It contains relatively comprehensive and extremely detailed information on family resources, incomes, overall production, consumption, and marketing -- a subset of variables included in the annual survey needed to estimate family incomes and consumption.

The household data covers 276 counties (out of 2,300) in all 25 provinces (or minority autonomous regions) and three municipal cities. The sample contained 48.4% pure farming households, 30.7% part-farming households, and 20.9% non-farming households. The "poor counties" were represented in about 20% of the total observations.

Comparing the provincial average per capita incomes estimated from the subsample with similar estimates for the entire SSB survey, the discrepancy was within 5% in all but four provinces. However, for smaller geographic units, such as counties, some bias is found due to small sample size. This should not affect estimation of cross-sectional statistical relationships.

Data Limitations

Selection of survey variables for inclusion in the income distribution survey left much to be desired from the viewpoint of estimating a full household model. The data set includes:

(a) Income: all components of real and cash income (including deductions necessary to derive net from gross income in certain categories);

(b) Production: production and sales (with corresponding prices) for every major crop and animal product; cultivated and irrigated area, but not area by crop; total cost of production (including cash purchase and self-supplied) and cash purchases of most farming inputs (not including labor); and capital assets (production inputs and costs are not broken down by product);

(c) Consumption: a nearly complete grain supply-demand balance is enumerated (stocks or changes in stock are omitted; feed data for about one-third of families is subsumed within coarse grain consumption rather separately listed, as indicated by animal production without corresponding feed entries); cash expenditure on total, staple and non-staple foods; but purchases of foods other than grain are omitted, so that only production minus sales can be used to estimate consumption of nongrain food items (this is a good approximation for items like vegetables in which almost all farm families are self-sufficient, but poor for livestock products like pork or beef, for which most families rely on the market for most consumption, due to perishability of product). Data on non-food (cash) consumption expenditures are absent.

(d) Household characteristics: only family size, indicators of the geographic location (plains, hilly or mountainous areas; poverty areas; suburban or rural; etc). No indication of family labor force, age, or health status.

(e) Prices: quota, negotiated, and market prices for sales of all items; resale and market purchase prices for grain; prices of all major inputs; but no price of non-agricultural consumption goods.

(f) Wealth: values and physical quantities of end-year stock of most major "lumpy"items of expenditure, including housing and capital equipment, but no consumer durables; various financial assets (deposits, debts, etc., as end-year stocks, but not flows).

No data is included on labor or wages (except aggregate incomes from non-farm or off-farm activities). Also, as the data is cross-sectional, there are no indicators of price or production variability or risk.

The data set, as first encountered, was not very "clean", and the definitional relationships among various variables unclear. Although the sample was drawn from the SSB's data tapes as a subset of the annual rural household survey data set, the individual observations contain numerous errors and omissions, due presumably to careless recording and inadequate checking. Only a part of the variables recorded in the entire survey were included, namely those of main interest to an income distribution study. Although the entire survey includes a number of full balance tables for each household (income and expenditure, origin and uses of grain, etc.), making it relatively easy to check for inconsistencies, the subsample contains no complete balances and even deviates from the official definitions of variables in some cases. This made it difficult to perform consistency checks, clean the data, or interpret it. At the end, about one-fourth of the households had to be dropped from the data for any given type of econometric analysis, because of incomplete or grossly inaccurate data (most of these were presumably rural residents with non-farm occupations).

Some items of importance can be estimated. For example, feed requirements can be roughly split out from coarse grain, where it has been omitted, by regression analysis relating feed (where recorded) and livestock production. Caloric content of the diet can be estimated with some error due to omission of cash purchases (e.g., of meat). A published rural survey data set for Hunan, which was complete in variables and aggregated data either by income groups or counties (nearly 100 observations), was used to evaluate various methods of estimating variables omitted from the national survey data set, as well as to gain an understanding of the quantitative significance of such omissions. However, the omissions of expenditures and various kinds of financial flow data from the national data set gives no basis for estimating important missing variables such as non-food expenditures and their prices or labor and wages. Fortunately, measures of poverty, commercialization, and food security can be easily assembled from the data.

Omission of starting and ending stocks of grain, other commodities, and financial assets and liabilities also makes it impossible to reconcile balance sheets (for foodgrain, feed, and financial assets, where inflows and outflows do not necessarily balance). Models such as Strauss' (1986) ignore the significance of changes in stocks or asset positions to farm households, effectively treating them as a source of random error. Although we must do the same for want of relevant data, it became apparent that these can be very large, not entirely random (e.g., most households in regions experiencing a good crop year will tend to accumulate stocks, and vice versa) and probably are quite strong exogenous influences on farm decision making for marketing and consumption.

The inclusion in the data set of rather complete breakdowns of sales and purchases at different prices (quota, negotiated, market, and resale) makes the household model which accounts for administrative pricing and quotas potentially appropriate for estimation purposes. The existence of a wage labor market in China in 1988 means that separability can be assumed, even though absence of labor variables from the data forces the exclusion of labor-leisure relationships from the model.

Means of Variables.

Because the large size of the data set provides adequate degrees of freedom, it was possible to estimate each equation or equation set for households grouped into categories relevant to the issues being examined -- income (poverty) and food security (commercialization is taken as an endogenous property, the result of family decisions). The groupings were by (a) per capita net income quintiles; (b) poor and non-poor counties (as officially defined -- see Chapter III); (c) food self-sufficiency (production of all foods *less than* or *greater than* 2,400 KCal/day per capita); (d) food consumption adequacy (*less than* or *greater than* 2,400 KCal/day per capita); and (e) "doubly insecure" (neither self-sufficient nor adequate, with both production and consumption less than 2,400 KCal). The last three are various ways of distinguishing the food insecure from the food secure families based only on available sample data. The 2,400 KCal criterion is the official standard of nutritional adequacy (Chapter III). Note that availability of a single year's data do not allow us to distinguish chronic food insecurity from transitory insecurity.

The hypothesis that the coefficients collectively do not differ by income or food security groups was tested using an F-test[15]. For all groupings employed and equations or equation sets, this hypothesis was rejected at 5% or better levels

---

[15] $[(SSE_R - SSE)/SSE][dof/(dof_R-dof)]$, where R indicates the restriction that coefficients are equal across groupings, and SSE is the total sum of squares from the grouped regressions, is distributed as F with $dof/(dof_R-dof)$ degrees of freedom.

of significance. Therefore the division by income and/or food security groups is meaningful.

The arithmetic means of variables used in the supply and demand function regressions are shown in Table 5.1a-b.[16] A number of interesting relationships can be observed from simple correlations or differences in group means (all statements below reflect evaluation of correlations of variables with per capita income, or tests of differences between group means, evaluated at the 5% level):

- staple food supply per capita increases with increased per capita income; it is higher for non-poor than poor, and for food secure than insecure, on all measures;

- the average county (market) prices of staple food are not significantly different across any groups -- including poor and non-poor counties; although the price differences for some cash crops do differ significantly between groups, the direction of differences is not systematic across crops;

- cultivated land per household is surprisingly uniform across all groups (although the poorest have significantly more land than others); but quality, as measured by irrigated percentage, is not uniform: the richer in income, the residents of non-poor counties, and the food secure all are characterized by significantly higher percentages of irrigated land.

---

[16] As the means of logarithms, i.e., the log-geometric means, were used in actual regressions, predictions of staple food supply based on arithmetic means differs slightly from the arithmetic mean of actual staple food supply.

Similar relationships for fertilizer and fixed capital indicate different overall levels of production inputs for the poor/non-poor or food secure/insecure;

- as one would expect, increased per capita income is associated with decreased average household size; similarly, households in poor areas and households who are food insecure tend to have larger household sizes;

- however, the average incomes of the poor counties residents do not fall in the bottom-most income quintile, and the food insecure, by various measures, have average incomes close to that of the entire sample, and are in most respects better off than residents of poor counties; the food consumption of residents in the poor counties are above the official standard of energy intake. The consumption of the bottom quintile is almost 2,100 KCal, which is higher than that of all three "food insecure" groups.

- the geographical distribution of the various income quintiles among regions varies as one would expect: the better-off regions have a higher proportion of the better-off households, and a higher proportion of rich households live in the plains than in the mountains; (most "poor counties" are located in the mountainous areas); and

- most interesting, the distribution of the "food insecure", however defined, among regions or types of area is not significantly different from the distribution of the "food secure". This calls into question the association of food insecurity with poverty in income or poverty areas, even though the poor and the food insecure share a weak productive base (low input levels).

Table 5.1a Means of Variables by Income Quintile

	Units	Total	Income Quintile				
			I	II	III	IV	V
Mean Income/P.C.	Yuan	568	241	385	509	666	1,150
Food Produced/P.C.	KCal	3,862	2,645	3,384	3,998	4,352	4,931
Food Consumed/P.C.	KCal	2,485	2,089	2,270	2,397	2,574	3,096
Staple Food Prod.	jin	5581	4291	5179	5934	6152	6350
Expenditure on:							
Staple Food	Yuan	1,022	933	1,017	1,038	1,046	1,074
Nonstaple Food	Yuan	809	545	680	785	903	1,129
Other Food	Yuan	202	358	102	127	167	253
Price: Staple Food	Y/jin	0.40	0.40	0.39	0.38	0.41	0.41
Price: Pork	"	2.35	2.27	2.30	2.32	2.34	2.43
Price: Vegetables	"	0.15	0.14	0.15	0.15	0.15	0.17
Price: Oilseeds	"	0.89	0.89	0.87	0.90	0.91	0.87
Price: Cotton	"	0.94	1.03	1.04	0.97	0.94	0.73
Price: Tobacco	"	0.79	0.82	0.80	0.72	0.73	0.83
Price: Jute/Hemp	"	0.34	0.42	0.39	0.34	0.30	0.26
Price: Sugar Crop	"	0.15	0.22	0.16	0.12	0.13	0.12
Cultivated Area	mu	11.88	14.30	11.68	10.52	11.69	11.19
Irrigated Area	%	0.48	0.32	0.44	0.49	0.55	0.61
Fixed Capital	Yuan	1619.55	1146.13	1214.16	1394.35	1606.03	2736.47
Price: Fertilizer	Y/jin	0.27	0.28	0.27	0.26	0.27	0.27
Household Size	nos.	5.08	5.53	5.37	5.12	4.87	4.49
Price: Nonstaples	Y/jin	2.15	1.97	2.03	2.16	2.25	2.32
Price: Other Food	Y/jin	0.46	0.48	0.51	0.50	0.43	0.39
Net Farm Income	Yuan	2708.79	1222.52	1940.47	2436.13	3052.20	4890.24
Exogenous Income	"	173.42	110.48	128.55	161.15	196.13	270.72
Region 1 (dummy)		0.03	0.00	0.01	0.01	0.02	0.10
Region 2		0.14	0.05	0.08	0.11	0.14	0.33
Region 4		0.38	0.58	0.47	0.39	0.33	0.15
Region 5		0.06	0.11	0.08	0.05	0.03	0.02
Plains (dummy)		0.45	0.32	0.39	0.44	0.52	0.59
Hilly (dummy)		0.34	0.34	0.36	0.38	0.32	0.28
Fertilizer Use	kgs/ha		382	576	741	694	767

Notes: 1 jin (catty) = 0.5 kg; 1 mu = 1/15 ha. Dummy values are proportions of subsample having 1 for each dummy; i.e., proportion belonging to each region/area. Region 3 and Mountainous areas are base conditions, reflected in regression intercept term. Mean Income/p.c., Food Produced/p.c., and Food Consumed/p.c. are related to differentiation of groups, but are not variables in regressions; nor is Fertilizer Use (kgs/ha, product weight), supplied as a reference variable only.

Table 5.1b <u>Means of Variables by Different Groups</u>

	County Status		Food Self-Sufficiency		Food Adequacy		Doubly Insecure
	Poor	Non-Poor	Sufficient	Insufficient	Adequate	Inadequate	
Mean Income/P.C.	405	611	594	517	619	534	494
Food Produced/P.C.	2,805	4,125	5,034	1,351	4,656	3,266	1,342
Food Consumed/P.C.	2,411	2,504	2,714	1,994	3,587	1,657	1,500
Staple Food Prod.	4265	5919	6453	3669	6105	5188	3831
Expenditure on:							
Staple Food	980	1,032	1,101	852	1,276	831	765
Nonstaple Food	689	839	837	749	909	733	707
Other Food	115	223	219	164	151	240	153
Price: Staple Food	0.40	0.40	0.40	0.40	0.38	0.41	0.41
Price: Pork	2.16	2.41	2.33	2.42	2.35	2.37	2.43
Price: Vegetables	0.13	0.16	0.15	0.15	0.15	0.15	0.15
Price: Oilseeds	0.78	0.91	0.88	0.91	0.89	0.89	0.90
Price: Cotton	0.75	0.99	0.95	0.93	0.95	0.93	0.89
Price: Tobacco	0.99	0.72	0.58	1.21	0.69	0.85	1.19
Price: Jute/Hemp	0.46	0.31	0.34	0.35	0.34	0.34	0.36
Price: Sugar Crop	0.21	0.13	0.09	0.28	0.15	0.15	0.26
Cultivated Area	11.17	12.07	11.81	12.03	11.03	12.52	11.70
Irrigated Area	0.28	0.53	0.53	0.37	0.51	0.46	0.38
Fixed Capital	1137.66	1732.97	1680.24	1486.28	1604.92	1630.56	1485.45
Price: Fertilizer	0.28	0.27	0.26	0.29	0.26	0.28	0.29
Household Size	5.30	5.02	4.98	5.29	4.81	5.27	5.40
Price: Nonstaples	2.02	2.18	2.09	2.27	2.06	2.21	2.32
Price: Other Food	0.53	0.45	0.42	0.55	0.48	0.45	0.54
Net Farm Income	1979.75	2889.72	2787.20	2540.70	2787.87	2649.34	2491.18
Exogenous Income	162.19	176.21	169.08	182.72	187.35	162.95	179.11
Region 1 (dummy)	0.01	0.03	0.02	0.04	0.03	0.03	0.03
Region 2	0.04	0.17	0.14	0.15	0.14	0.14	0.15
Region 4	0.61	0.33	0.36	0.43	0.37	0.40	0.44
Region 5	0.15	0.03	0.05	0.06	0.07	0.05	0.05
Plains (dummy)	0.15	0.53	0.49	0.38	0.42	0.48	0.40
Hilly (dummy)	0.32	0.34	0.36	0.29	0.37	0.31	0.29
Fertilizer Use	436	884	714	409	743	535	422

The means of variables used in estimation of feed demand are listed in Table 5.2a-b. These means, and the estimated equations, exclude households where animals were raised but no use of feedgrain was recorded (presumably omitted data). Variation of feed use among income and other groups is as might be expected. Feed use is about 20% of total grain production on average and ranged from 15-23% over various groups, with low income households, poor area residents, and the food insecure having lower feed use and lower livestock product production than other groups. Draft animal numbers relate more closely to the area cultivated, which does not vary much over our groupings.

Table 5.2a Feed Equation: Variable Means by Income Quintile

	Total	Income Quintile				
		I	II	III	IV	V
Feed Consumption	949.47	697.00	853.30	941.53	1051.06	1204.29
Hogs Fattened	2.80	1.12	1.32	2.95	1.60	7.17
Pork Produced	185.64	106.68	184.46	178.46	220.00	241.66
Draft Animals	0.05	0.04	0.04	0.07	0.05	0.04
Poultry	10.43	6.25	8.01	9.33	11.05	18.05
Eggs	51.71	27.57	32.48	37.74	88.48	74.27
Hogs^2	2443.63	224.74	135.19	2253.82	43.55	9736.27
Pork^2	303448	32339	1133767	87448	118253	173828
Draft Animals^2	0.15	0.06	0.12	0.44	0.10	0.07
Poultry^2	2759	353.12	928.18	547.53	1382.44	10771.49
Egg^2	556752	9010	4252	12285	2637510	161579
Pork/Feed Price	7.96	8.07	8.15	8.07	8.26	7.94
Region 1 Dummy	0.02	0.00	0.01	0.01	0.01	0.08
Region 2	0.12	0.04	0.07	0.10	0.13	0.25
Region 4	0.42	0.61	0.51	0.43	0.38	0.19
Region 5	0.06	0.11	0.08	0.04	0.04	0.02
Plains	0.45	0.32	0.38	0.43	0.53	0.55
Hilly	0.32	0.33	0.35	0.37	0.30	0.30

Table 5.2b Feed Equation: Variable Means by Different Groups

	County Status		Food Self-Sufficiency		Food Adequacy		Doubly
	Poor	Non-poor	Sufficient	Insufficient	Adequate	Inadequate	Insecure
Feed Consumption	772.27	996.44	1037.73	754.53	1102.53	841.69	717.41
Hogs Fattened	1.70	3.09	3.01	2.35	4.92	1.32	1.29
Pork Produced	232.27	173.27	199.16	155.76	226.60	156.80'	147.67
Draft Animals	0.07	0.04	0.05	0.05	0.06	0.04	0.04
Poultry	7.97	11.08	11.70	7.61	11.28	9.82	7.95
Eggs	27.72	58.08	59.62	34.26	78.41	32.92	25.79
Hogs^2	248.36	3025.69	2783.00	1693.00	5689.00	158.65	282.58
Pork^2	1097519	92903	409111	70111	634276	70542	63415
Draft Animal^2	0.42	0.08	0.17	0.12	0.26	0.08	0.12
Poultry^2	481	3363	3708	664	1904	3361	786
Egg^2	8311	702170	782772	57625	1325885	15275	2110
Pork/Feed Price	8.13	7.91	7.82	8.27	8.11	7.85	8.22
Region 1 Dummy	0.01	0.03	0.02	0.04	0.03	0.02	0.02
Region 2	0.05	0.14	0.11	0.15	0.11	0.13	0.16
Region 4	0.62	0.36	0.41	0.43	0.43	0.41	0.43
Region 5	0.14	0.04	0.05	0.07	0.08	0.05	0.05
Plains	0.12	0.53	0.48	0.37	0.41	0.47	0.39
Hilly	0.31	0.33	0.34	0.28	0.35	0.31	0.28

C. Estimation Results

The model was estimated as a combination of a supply function (foodgrains only), three consumer demand functions (foodgrains, nonstaple foods, and other foods) were estimated simultaneously, and a feed grain demand function. Estimates for each equation were obtained for each data grouping, as described above. The elasticities of marketed supply with respect to price and income, the variable of most policy interest, are derived arithmetically from the supply and demand elasticities.

<u>Supply Function</u>

The results of the supply function regressions (estimated for variables in logarithmic form) are shown in Tables 5.3a-b. R-squares were around 0.40 for all of the log equations. T-statistics of all parameters shown in parentheses were mostly significant at the 5% level or better.

The magnitudes and signs of the own-price supply elasticities are, as expected, mostly positive; however, they are uniformly low and most are not statistically significant. Previous studies for other developing countries have found own-price elasticities to be typically higher than the 0.02-0.05 found here for China, with a short-run response elsewhere in the range 0.1-0.8 (Tsakok, 1990). The weak supply response is consistent with the hypotheses derived in Section IV from the two models involving quota procurement and pricing and a "price wedge" respectively: <u>both the quota system and a price wedge between selling and buying prices would</u> <u>cause a certain number of farmers to choose "corner solutions"</u>, that is, to produce no more food grain than necessary to meet quota sales requirement and own consumption demand. One would expect to find no systematic correlation between prices and amount supplied for the subsample of farmers whose supply optima are not internal solutions, and this would reduce magnitude and significance of estimated coefficients of supply response in regressions on a sample with farmers at both internal and border solutions. In fact, in our data set, some 47% of households have no *voluntary* sales of grain at all, and presumably are therefore at corner solutions. The range is from 41% for the self-sufficient group (whose production more than meets consumption requirements) to 57% for the insufficient group, 51% for both the top income quintile and the poor areas group. As stated above, the Tobit estimation procedure would be the ideal method for estimation in this situation, but had to be rejected for want of adequate software.

Cross-price elasticities are mostly of the expected negative sign and small in magnitude, except for the elasticity with respect to vegetable prices (pork prices are an exception in having positive sign in many cases, because grain is a major input into pork production). A majority of the coefficients are statistically significant. Overall, a doubling of all cash crop prices would reduce grain supply by only 15%, and most of this is attributable to vegetables, which is the main source of free market activity. Lower or zero cross-price supply elasticities have often been found for other developing countries (*SSS*, 1986). Again, the Chinese experience in the early 1980s was that farmers have responded to improved relative prices of cash crops (official procurement prices for cash crops, relative to declining market prices for grain) by shifting acreage into those crops (for example, cotton in Shandong). However, in these cases, reduced grain acreage was more than offset by increased grain yields, so that production of staple food did not fall. Therefore, again this experience is not inconsistent with our findings.

Therefore, the hypothesis that supply positively responds to own-price variation and negatively to cross-price are accepted. However, it is more interesting to look at the difference of responses among different groups.

Regarding the distinctions among poor/non-poor and food secure/insecure, it was previously noted that the characteristics of the groups identified as food insecure were different from those of the poor. From the regression results, this is also shown: although the poor on the whole are less price-responsive than the non-poor (judging by sign, size, and significance of direct and cross-price coefficients), farmers who are not self-sufficient in food, or who consume less than the 2,400 KCal per day, or both (the "doubly insecure") all seem more price-responsive than the food secure. Even though the magnitude of own-price elasticities for all groups are small, three "food insecure" groups have relatively higher own-price elasticities. But, for the cross-price elasticities, these three groups also exhibit different responses. For example, the cross-price elasticities to pork price are negative for the food insecure rather than positive, as they are with other groups. The positive cross-price elasticity to pork is to be expected if the increased grain is to be used for feed rather than human consumption. However, the "food insecure" groups appear less interested in raising pigs than in human consumption -- we have seen above that they have low feed use (less livestock production than other groups; see Table 5.2b). Furthermore, these three groups have higher (more negative) cross-price elasticities to oil seed and vegetables than other groups, perhaps implying that the "food insecure" include a high proportion of profit-oriented farmers, as opposed to subsistence-oriented farmers. On the other hand, the grain production of the food insecure is not responsive to price variation for other cash crops. We suppose that, whereas oilseeds and vegetables can be grown with decent yields almost anywhere, other cash crops tend to be strongly region-specific, so that relative scarcity (high prices) does not result cross-sectionally in adjustments in crop area. The poor (bottom quintile) have behaviour similar to the three "food insecure" groups, but not the poor counties.

Variables other than prices also affect the output supply. In the models, the main production function parameters -- land, labor (proxy), fixed capital, and fertilizer (represented by its price) -- show correct signs, reasonable magnitudes, and low standard errors permitting rather narrow confidence intervals. Land and irrigation are particularly important factors. The irrigation percentage allows us to distinguish land quality: on average, based on the formula given above, the marginal productivity of irrigated land is estimated to be 1.76 times that of non-irrigated land on average. That ratio proves highest among the poor (bottom quintile) and in the poor counties (2.22 and 2.04 respectively), probably due to concentration of poverty in arid areas or hilly/mountainous areas where unirrigated land is steeply sloped.

Table 5.3a Results of Supply Regressions by Income Quintile

	Total	Income Quintile				
		I	II	III	IV	V
Constant	5.635 (90.18)	5.2330 (41.08)	5.6546 (43.46)	6.0045 (42.57)	5.6686 (39.35)	6.082 (39.23)
Grain Price	0.0192 (1.68)	0.0082 (0.36)	-0.0176 (0.75)	0.0257 (0.99)	0.0234 (0.93)	0.0490 (1.69)
Pork Price	0.0032 (1.15)	-0.0143 (1.61)	-0.0022 (0.25)	0.0133 (1.62)	0.0213 (2.38)	0.0001 (0.01)
Vegetable Price	-0.1019 (8.68)	-0.1516 (6.00)	-0.0790 (3.29)	-0.0658 (2.41)	-0.1029 (3.99)	-0.1021 (3.77)
Rapeseed Price	-0.0039 (4.47)	-0.0036 (0.84)	0.0015 (0.34)	-0.0162 (3.38)	-0.0142 (3.00)	-0.0123 (2.65)
Cotton Price	-0.0115 (8.26)	-0.0132 (4.62)	-0.0037 (1.29)	-0.0060 (2.02)	-0.0088 (2.80)	-0.0148 (4.17)
Sugarcane Price	-0.0032 (1.91)	-0.0029 (0.82)	-0.0040 (1.10)	-0.0037 (0.95)	-0.0010 (2.46)	-0.0074 (1.62)
Tobacco Price	-0.0100 (6.35)	-0.0184 (6.07)	-0.0140 (4.49)	-0.0121 (3.70)	-0.0092 (2.66)	-0.0014 (0.39)
Jute/Hemp Price	-0.0070 (4.56)	-0.0082 (2.78)	-0.0035 (1.14)	-0.0004 (0.11)	-0.0099 (2.81)	-0.0020 (0.50)
Cultivated Area	0.4138 (44.75)	0.2015 (11.13)	0.3402 (16.07)	0.4364 (20.36)	0.4835 (22.86)	0.5633 (28.38)
Irrigated Percentage	0.2381 (13.95)	0.1832 (4.87)	0.1690 (4.55)	0.1247 (3.29)	0.1914 (4.82)	0.3177 (8.19)
Fixed Capital	0.0518 (9.68)	0.0622 (5.51)	0.0514 (4.36)	0.0334 (2.62)	0.0519 (4.18)	0.0104 (0.85)
Fertilizer Price	-0.2120 (11.76)	-0.2832 (8.17)	-0.2199 (6.00)	-0.1521 (3.76)	-0.1404 (3.21)	-0.1173 (2.64)
Household Size	0.4098 (19.97)	0.6756 (16.58)	0.5548 (12.58)	0.4394 (9.45)	0.3834 (7.78)	0.2754 (5.68)
Region 1 Dummy	-2593 (6.54)	-0.4409 (2.00)	-0.3263 (2.01)	-0.4266 (2.91)	-0.3209 (3.09)	-0.1706 (2.98)
Region 2 Dummy	0.1551 (7.61)	0.2205 (3.40)	0.1963 (3.73)	0.1590 (3.36)	0.1119 (2.56)	0.1694 (4.35)
Region 4 Dummy	-0.0804 (5.19)	-0.1352 (4.07)	-0.0254 (0.81)	-0.0706 (2.13)	-0.0280 (0.80)	0.0448 (0.95)
Region 5 Dummy	-0.2295 (7.94)	-0.2193 (4.39)	-0.1997 (3.78)	-0.1077 (1.57)	-0.0041 (0.05)	-0.0376 (0.31)
Plains Dummy	0.2443 (13.53)	0.2347 (6.59)	0.1388 (3.82)	0.2077 (5.19)	0.2066 (5.05)	0.2286 (4.87)
Hilly Area Dummy	0.2948 (16.44)	0.2433 (7.56)	0.2094 (6.04)	0.3029 (7.71)	0.2970 (6.80)	0.2671 (5.26)
R^2 (adj.)	0.40	0.40	0.37	0.39	0.44	0.47
DOF (error)	7947	1572	1574	1574	1573	1574
SSE	2393	372	390	435	477	540

Note: Absolute values of T-ratios in parentheses; boldface > 10% level significance.

Table 5.3b Results of Supply Regressions by Different Groups

	County Status		Food Self-Sufficiency		Food Adequacy		Doubly Insecure
	Poor	Non-poor	Sufficient	Insufficient	Adequate	Inadequate	
Constant	5.2778	5.8233	5.6347	5.7083	5.5883	5.7648	5.6464
	(35.00)	**(82.01)**	**(90.18)**	**(45.74)**	**(60.58)**	**(68.89)**	**(39.64)**
Grain Price	0.0119	0.0217	0.0075	0.0373	0.0009	0.0438	0.0347
	(0.49)	**(1.65)**	(0.76)	(1.64)	(0.05)	**(3.03)**	(1.44)
Pork Price	0.0058	0.0054	0.0088	-0.0090	0.0021	-0.0013	-0.0068
	(0.67)	**(1.81)**	**(3.66)**	(1.59)	(0.40)	(0.41)	(0.82)
Vegetable Price	-0.0633	-0.0987	-0.0593	-0.1493	-0.0772	-0.1047	-0.1430
	(2.05)	**(7.63)**	**(5.83)**	**(6.43)**	**(4.52)**	**(6.72)**	**(5.30)**
Rapeseed Price	-0.0018	-0.0152	-0.0094	-0.0208	-0.0036	-0.0127	-0.0211
	(0.42)	**(6.34)**	**(5.02)**	**(5.34)**	(1.10)	**(4.77)**	**(4.88)**
Cotton Price	-0.0000	-0.0129	-0.0092	-0.0190	-0.0114	-0.0096	-0.0191
	(0.01)	**(8.36)**	**(7.60)**	**(7.04)**	**(5.44)**	**(5.30)**	**(6.19)**
Sugarcane Price	-0.0035	-0.0024	-0.0070	0.0207	-0.0096	-0.0067	0.0132
	(0.98)	(1.28)	**(4.29)**	**(6.22)**	**(3.45)**	**(3.00)**	**(3.59)**
Tobacco Price	-0.0148	-0.0062	-0.0018	-0.0019	-0.0114	-0.0124	-0.0034
	(3.95)	**(3.49)**	(1.36)	(0.64)	**(5.44)**	**(6.22)**	(1.03)
Jute/Hemp Price	-0.0021	-0.0068	-0.0097	0.0064	-0.0126	-0.0006	0.0118
	(0.62)	**(3.83)**	**(7.29)**	**(2.13)**	**(5.61)**	(0.30)	**(3.49)**
Cultivated Area	0.3606	0.4202	0.2862	0.3851	0.4004	0.4060	0.4024
	(18.29)	**(39.70)**	**(30.95)**	**(24.56)**	**(27.39)**	**(34.66)**	**(22.13)**
Irrigated Percentage	0.2989	0.2219	0.1221	0.1042	0.2807	0.1566	0.0973
	(5.92)	**(11.93)**	**(7.99)**	**(3.00)**	**(10.56)**	**(6.97)**	**(2.52)**
Fixed Capital	0.0613	0.0492	0.0429	0.0059	0.0254	0.0542	0.0216
	(4.56)	**(8.38)**	**(8.84)**	(0.60)	**(3.02)**	**(8.06)**	**(2.05)**
Fertilizer Price	-0.4841	-0.1452	-0.1227	-0.1073	-0.2964	-0.0880	-0.1224
	(12.16)	**(7.06)**	**(7.60)**	**(3.00)**	**(10.66)**	**(3.66)**	**(2.96)**
Household Size	0.4746	0.4005	0.5693	0.5634	0.5277	0.4186	0.5141
	(10.75)	**(17.34)**	**(30.87)**	**(14.25)**	**(17.43)**	**(15.17)**	**(11.35)**
Region 1 Dummy	0.2342	-0.2739	-0.1361	-0.1375	-0.1982	-0.2391	-0.0660
	(1.53)	**(6.61)**	**(3.58)**	**(2.03)**	**(3.40)**	**(4.50)**	(0.80)
Region 2 Dummy	0.1547	0.1421	0.0793	0.2969	0.1208	0.1774	0.2960
	(2.00)	**(6.69)**	**(4.45)**	**(7.41)**	**(4.05)**	**(6.60)**	**(6.67)**
Region 4 Dummy	-0.0619	-0.0548	-0.0492	-0.1600	-0.0242	-0.0906	-0.1452
	(1.27)	**(3.23)**	**(3.56)**	**(5.18)**	(1.00)	**(4.52)**	**(4.26)**
Region 5 Dummy	-0.2319	-0.0581	-0.2075	-0.2707	-0.1905	-0.2261	-0.2857
	(3.61)	(1.47)	**(8.04)**	**(4.87)**	**(4.59)**	**(5.58)**	**(4.21)**
Plains Dummy	0.2596	0.1947	0.1662	0.1651	0.2695	0.2500	0.1682
	(5.90)	**(8.52)**	**(9.83)**	**(5.05)**	**(9.62)**	**(10.85)**	**(4.69)**
Hilly Area Dummy	0.2446	0.2524	0.1809	0.1863	0.2923	0.2926	0.1974
	(7.33)	**(10.80)**	**(10.60)**	**(5.85)**	**(10.83)**	**(12.54)**	**(5.57)**
R^2 (adj.)	0.43	0.39	0.46	0.41	0.41	0.42	0.41
DOF (error)	1517	6283	5454	2473	3401	4526	1874
SSE	438	1867	855	868	953	1312	622

Note: Absolute values of T-ratios in parentheses; boldface > 10% level significance.

Fertilizer does not enter the model directly, but the estimated coefficient for fertilizer prices can be converted to an estimation of elasticity with respect to fertilizer input [since $\beta_4 = -\beta_z/(1-\beta_z)$ in the supply model, $\beta_z = \beta_4/(\beta_4-1)$]. On average, the fertilizer elasticity (calculated) was 0.175; it is inversely related to income quintiles, and is highest in the poor counties (0.326). It should be noted that, if the hypothesized model is correct (that is, optimization of supply with respect to fertilizer use), the estimated coefficients on land, capital, and labor are not the actual elasticity coefficients, but the latter must be divided by $(1-\beta_z)$, where β_z is the estimated elasticity with respect to fertilizer.

Table 5.4 shows the calculated production function elasticities. Across income groups, the elasticity with respect to land rises with income and all other input elasticities correspondingly decline. The scale coefficient (sum of elasticities) indicates strong increasing returns to scale for the poorest (both the poor and the poor areas), declining to nearly constant returns to scale for the richest. Overall, these coefficients suggest that grain production technology is input-intensive for the poorest, and becomes more extensive for the richest (this does not mean, for example, that the poor use more fertilizer or labor per hectare, but that, for the same input intensities, the ratios of the marginal productivities of fertilizer or labor to that of land will be higher for the poor; or, for the same relative factor prices, the optimum factor proportions for the poor will be more input intensive). The presence of substantial returns to scale at low income levels, even though average household size does not differ much, may suggest that the poor have more fragmented land (with many small plots) than the rich, who have already consolidated their land; and/or that wealthier farmers may have to hire wage labor, which is usually less productive than family labor.

The differences in supply functions for poor and non-poor are potentially very important for policy makers. Approaches other than price policy, such as providing technology assistance, improving rural infrastructure (irrigation) and supplying more modern inputs, may be appropriately used to target needy farmers, as we have seen that the poor are not very price responsive, but the marginal productivity of inputs such as fertilizer or irrigation tends to be higher than for richer farmers. On the other hand, the "food insecure" group appear price-responsive, but not input-responsive. These observations also suggest there is no economic sacrifice involved in targeting the poor (rather than the rich) for either productivity-improving investment or subsidized input supply. Rather, this may raise overall economic efficiency.

Table 5.4 Supply Function Elasticities

	Fertilizer	Labor	Land	Capital	Scale Coefficient
Total	0.175	0.497	0.502	0.063	1.236
Quintile I	0.221	0.867	0.259	0.080	1.426
Quintile II	0.180	0.677	0.415	0.063	1.335
Quintile III	0.132	0.506	0.503	0.038	1.179
Quintile IV	0.123	0.437	0.551	0.059	1.171
Quintile V	0.105	0.308	0.629	0.012	1.054
Poor Counties					
Poor	0.326	0.704	0.535	0.091	1.657
Non-Poor	0.127	0.459	0.481	0.056	1.123
Food Self-Sufficiency					
Sufficient	0.109	0.639	0.321	0.048	1.118
Insufficient	0.097	0.624	0.426	0.006	1.154
Consumption Adequacy					
Adequate	0.229	0.684	0.519	0.033	1.465
Inadequate	0.081	0.455	0.442	0.059	1.037
Doubly Insecure	0.109	0.577	0.452	0.024	1.162

The signs and magnitudes of the regional dummy variables shown in the Table 5.3a-b prove consistent with the expected productivity rankings of the groups of provinces, with one exception: the suburbs of Beijing, Shanghai, and Tianjin (region I) have the lowest productivity ranking. This may be partly because the major part of the household labor force in the suburbs is not engaged in agriculture, contrary to the assumption by which household size is taken as a proxy for farm labor; so that the Region I dummy may be biased downwards to offset the overprediction of grain output based on the household size proxy. As expected, productivity in the plains and hilly areas is higher than in the mountains, but, surprisingly, productivity in the plains is below that in the hilly areas. Since the equation variables already account for the influence of irrigation, fertilizer use, etc. (all higher in the plains), perhaps the hilly areas have an additional advantage in better drainage.

The unfavorability of environmental conditions for grain production in the poorer regions of China (Region V, including Gansu, Shaanxi, and Tibet; and the mountainous areas) can be seen by comparing the ratios of the regional dummies (in exponential form): productivity in Region V is about 70% of productivity in Region II (Jiangsu, Guangdong, Zhejiang, and Liaoning), other inputs being equal (including irrigation and fertilizer use). Similarly, productivity in the plains and hilly areas is 25% and 34% higher respectively than in the mountainous areas.

Consumer Demand Function

The estimated regression coefficients for the jointly-estimated QES consumer demand functions (1 - foodgrains, 2 - nonstaple foods, and 3 - other foods) are listed in Tables 5.5a-b. In general, R^2s are not very impressive, although most F-statistics are highly significant; R^2s are highest for the non-staple food equation, vary unsystematically among different groups, and are often low or zero for the "other foods" equation (probably because this category is so heterogeneous). However, most parameters estimated are significant at 5% level or better. The coefficients of variables across groups are reasonably consistent in signs. However, the signs and magnitudes of estimated coefficients are not able to tell us much about the estimated response to variations in price and income because of the complexity of the QES function. The price and income elasticities must be calculated from the

derivatives and mean values of variables, using the normal elasticity formula. These

are shown in Table 5.6 below.

Table 5.5a <u>Consumption Demand Equations: Estimated Parameters by Income Quintile</u>

	Total	I	II	III	IV	V
		--------------- Income Quintile -------------				
a_1	0.2054	0.4610	0.5421	0.4539	0.3324	0.1567
	(40.23)	(10.26)	(22.89)	(20.09)	(18.44)	(20.62)
a_2	0.1738	0.2627	0.3121	0.2943	0.2275	0.1810
	(38.11)	(8.08)	(14.14)	(16.85)	(14.48)	(25.07)
a_3	-0.0500	-0.2140	0.0666	0.0783	0.0544	0.0378
	(5.34)	(2.51)	(7.48)	(9.35)	(7.58)	(11.26)
c_1	143.1878	100.8971	30.6868	58.3992	64.6766	189.7354
	(5.86)	(1.78)	(0.46)	(0.65)	(1.02)	(3.21)
c_2	-8.6678	16.8888	37.3803	33.5833	49.7208	-0.1624
	(1.48)	(1.13)	(2.75)	(3.27)	(4.68)	(0.01)
c_3	89.8471	-248.6621	-14.4116	-15.9026	-23.2411	-5.2261
	(2.34)	(2.27)	(2.38)	(2.42)	(3.23)	(0.46)
δ_1	0.2054	0.4610	0.5421	0.4539	0.3324	0.1567
	(40.23)	(10.26)	(22.89)	(20.09)	(18.44)	(20.62)
δ_2	0.1738	0.2627	0.3121	0.2943	0.2275	0.1810
	(38.11)	(8.08)	(14.14)	(16.85)	(14.48)	(25.07)
δ_3	-0.0500	-0.2139	0.0666	0.0783	0.0544	0.0378
	(5.34)	(2.51)	(7.48)	(9.35)	(7.58)	(11.26)
ϵ	-123.2529	-41.1882	-10.1219	-17.3732	-39.8246	-130.2836
	(20.56)	(4.42)	(2.97)	(4.62)	(6.61)	(8.40)
r_1	-79.7308	-60.4945	-38.7106	7.4297	42.4714	101.9027
	(2.58)	(0.25)	(0.61)	(0.13)	(1.08)	(3.73)
r_2	150.7730	214.9089	56.4375	20.7762	62.9528	85.1777
	(10.02)	(3.20)	(3.01)	(1.15)	(3.76)	(4.87)
r_3	57.4650	-8.0472	-12.3889	-46.4935	-21.4185	-40.1318
	(5.61)	(0.27)	(1.20)	(3.91)	(1.67)	(1.84)
r_4	-3.6615	-96.7610	-59.4088	-132.5590	-80.3819	101.6640
	(0.17)	(2.07)	(3.16)	(4.95)	(2.50)	(1.65)
d_1	22.4430	9.3504	-26.6790	-58.9734	-28.7231	17.5416
	(1.99)	(0.29)	(2.27)	(4.47)	(2.01)	(0.97)
d_2	155.0773	108.7255	23.2379	16.3010	21.4284	16.2650
	(13.26)	(3.53)	(1.98)	(1.20)	(1.39)	(0.80)
R^2 (adjusted) /1	0.12/0.27 /0.00	0.12/0.19 /0.00	0.17/0.16 /0.00	0.23/0.26 /0.01	0.25/0.20 /0.03	0.14/0.20 /0.09
DOF	8027	1599	1602	1603	1601	1602
SSE (Grain)	3.1e-10	4.7e-09	4.6e-09	4.8e-09	5.2e-09	9.3e-09

/1 For the simultaneously-estimated equations: staple, non-staple, and "other" food.
T-statistics in parentheses; bold-face means significant at the 5% level or more.
The parameters in the table are matched the equation V.1 on page 160.

Table 5.5b <u>Consumption Demand Equations: Estimated Parameters by Different Groups</u>

	County Status		Food Self-sufficiency		Food Adequacy		Doubly Insecure
	Poor	Non-poor	Sufficiency	Insufficiency	Adequate	Inadequate	
a_1	0.3882 **(24.36)**	0.1865 **(33.68)**	0.2535 **(31.32)**	0.1462 **(26.66)**	0.2920 **(27.89)**	0.1295 **(26.46)**	0.1231 **(21.76)**
a_2	0.2537 **(17.67)**	0.1755 **(34.44)**	0.1901 **(27.93)**	0.1357 **(25.07)**	0.1942 **(24.15)**	0.1239 **(26.11)**	0.1226 **(21.56)**
a_3	0.0406 **(9.87)**	-0.0361 **(3.08)**	0.0333 **(2.24)**	0.0241 **(11.62)**	0.0254 **(8.38)**	-0.0142 (1.03)	0.0199 **(9.22)**
c_1	-46.0500 (1.10)	291.6766 **(9.24)**	222.4302 **(6.09)**	-4.6192 (0.16)	200.2598 **(3.65)**	46.7195 **(2.06)**	4.0948 (0.15)
c_2	9.3515 (0.64)	-8.0180 (1.24)	2.4431 (0.31)	-10.6368 (1.27)	12.5211 (1.10)	-17.9125 **(2.74)**	-12.6404 (1.51)
c_3	-17.6214 **(2.66)**	166.9769 **(3.86)**	170.8158 **(3.84)**	-11.1554 (1.81)	-24.6194 **(4.99)**	388.4859 **(5.95)**	-5.2746 (0.79)
δ_1	0.3881 **(24.36)**	0.1865 **(33.68)**	0.2535 **(31.32)**	0.1462 **(26.66)**	0.2920 **(27.89)**	0.1295 **(26.46)**	0.1231 **(21.76)**
δ_2	0.2537 **(17.67)**	0.1755 **(34.44)**	0.1901 **(27.93)**	0.1357 **(25.07)**	0.1942 **(24.15)**	0.1239 **(26.11)**	0.1226 **(21.56)**
δ_3	0.0406 **(9.87)**	-0.0361 **(3.08)**	0.0333 **(2.24)**	0.0241 **(11.62)**	0.0254 **(8.38)**	-0.0142 (1.03)	0.0199 **(9.22)**
ϵ	-54.0191 **(8.94)**	-123.3184 **(17.53)**	-110.4294 **(15.37)**	-184.2775 **(15.84)**	-136.3338 **(17.08)**	-193.7468 **(17.18)**	-197.1474 **(13.95)**
r_1	310.6172 **(7.69)**	-61.7137 (1.85)	-97.9444 **(2.35)**	122.1826 **(4.84)**	96.4386 **(4.13)**	40.6793 (1.11)	86.1017 **(2.86)**
r_2	55.3853 **(2.42)**	152.5327 **(9.48)**	171.6614 **(9.23)**	102.8077 **(7.35)**	51.9065 **(4.28)**	211.4142 **(12.47)**	122.8383 **(8.31)**
r_3	11.9583 (1.38)	50.9904 **(4.13)**	69.5213 **(5.45)**	-2.0336 (0.21)	9.7386 (1.18)	75.3780 **(6.39)**	0.0778 (0.01)
r_4	-24.9265 **(2.00)**	-46.7550 (1.50)	-19.3797 (0.73)	-31.5680 (1.64)	-53.7582 **(3.52)**	26.6302 (1.01)	-46.7089 **(1.97)**
d_1	-0.0363 (0.00)	37.0750 **(2.75)**	-29.7491 **(2.05)**	20.8052 **(2.02)**	9.1847 (0.98)	44.5762 **(3.48)**	21.5055 (1.95)
d_2	5.7073 (0.64)	166.1509 **(11.56)**	141.9863 **(9.58)**	33.8509 **(3.09)**	49.3270 **(5.33)**	131.7591 **(9.53)**	29.4232 **(2.47)**
R^2 (adjusted) /1	0.09/0.23 /0.15	0.13/0.27 /0.00	0.14/0.28 /0.00	0.12/0.27 /0.11	0.12/0.25 /0.10	0.21/0.29 /0.00	0.17/0.31 /0.11
DOF	1592	6357	5472	2550	3442	4580	1927
SSE (Grain)	5.7e-09	2.5e-10	2.2e-10	7.3e-09	1.5e-10	1.1e-10	4.6e-09

/1 For the simultaneously-estimated equations: staple, non-staple, and "other" food.
T-statistics in parentheses; bold-face means significant at the 5% level or more.

Table 5.6 <u>Estimated Demand Elasticities By Group</u>

| | Elasticity of Staple Food Demand with respect to: | | | | | | Staple Food | |
| | Grain Price | | Non-staple Price | | | | | |
	Without Profit Effect	With Profit Effect	Without Profit Effect	With Profit Effect	Other Food Price	Income	Consump tion Per Capita	Expend iture %
Total	-0.760	-0.430	0.346	0.363	0.086	0.491	248	34.6
Quintile I	0.550	0.015	0.386	0.415	0.233	0.550	210	69.3
Quintile II	-0.621	0.097	0.252	0.288	0.046	0.832	251	50.8
Quintile III	-0.727	-0.162	0.236	0.262	0.047	0.717	284	42.5
Quintile IV	-0.767	-0.302	0.257	0.280	0.053	0.683	282	34.7
Quintile V	-0.790	-0.506	0.276	0.293	0.054	0.610	283	20.2
Poor Counties								
Poor	-0.759	-0.335	0.306	0.332	0.070	0.590	241	47.2
Non-Poor	-0.713	-0.387	0.328	0.344	0.076	0.472	259	33.7
Food Self-Sufficiency								
Sufficient	-0.746	-0.366	0.313	0.331	0.062	0.489	286	38.2
Insufficient	-0.808	-0.586	0.430	0.452	0.102	0.444	193	29.8
Consumption Adequacy								
Adequate	-0.735	-0.420	0.315	0.335	0.069	0.497	358	44.2
Inadequate	-0.804	-0.513	0.418	0.431	0.080	0.419	184	28.2
Doubly Insecure	-0.827	-0.611	0.427	0.439	0.098	0.394	161	26.7

As discussed in Chapter II, agricultural household models differ from ordinary consumer demand models in the inclusion of a "profit effect", which indicates how price changes affect demand, not only through the income and substitution effects, but also through changes in farm profits (which are part of income in the consumer demand equation). One of the testable hypotheses in the previous section was that the profit effect has substantial influence on consumption behavior. Thus the usual elasticity formula for the demand for the ith commodity with respect to the jth price, in this case can be written:

$$\frac{P_j}{C_i}\frac{\partial C_i}{\partial P_j} = \frac{P_j}{C_i}\frac{\partial C_i}{\partial P_j}\bigg|_{d\pi=0} + \frac{P_j}{C_i}\frac{\partial C_i}{\partial \pi}\frac{\partial \pi}{\partial P_j}$$, where π = farm profit = production revenue

less cost. Table 5.6 presents elasticities as measured by the first term of the formula

(profits constant) and as the sum of the two right-hand-side terms (profits variable).

Own-price elasticity of demand for staple food (excluding profit effect)

is negative across all groups. It varies from -0.55 to -0.83, demand becoming more

price elastic with increased income, as one would expect. The cross-price elasticity

of demand for staple food with respect to non-staple food price was uniformly

positive and ranged from 0.25-0.43; but the elasticity with respect to the price of

"other food" is rather minor. On the whole, the revealed consumption behaviour of

Chinese farmers seems rather "normal" -- not what one would expect of farmers

living at or near subsistence levels (low direct and cross-price elasticities for food),

and indicative of readiness to substitute other foods and non-food commodities for

staple foods (especially those such as vegetables and meat, in the non-staple food

category).

Aside from substitutability, the income elasticity of demand for staple

foods remains positive and quite high, declining only moderately over income groups

-- staple foods are clearly not inferior goods. The share of staple foods in total

consumer budgets is 69% for the lowest income group, falling to 20% for the highest.

Thus the income effect on demand from increases in staple food prices is substantial and declines only moderately with increased income. The income and substitution effects are in this case mutually reinforcing.

The profit effect for Chinese farmers, is very substantial among all groups, enough to considerably reduce the magnitude of own-price elasticities and even reverse the sign among the lowest income groups. This is due to the large share of income from staple foods in total net farm income, plus the relatively small production effect calculated from the elasticity of supply with respect to price. The profit effect from non-staple food price increases is relatively small, and, from "other foods", so insignificant that it is ignored here. As a result, we accept the hypothesis that the poor, with high budget shares for food, have also high income elasticities of demand and low price elasticities of consumption. (Another hypothesis from the risk model, that the poor, with high budget share in food, are highly specialized in food production, cannot be confirmed due to lack of land allocation data.)

Comparing the findings for the poor/non-poor and several food secure/insecure categories, it is again clear (as on the supply side) that the food insecure are not the same as the poor in income or county of residence. With the poor/non-poor grouping, the behaviour of the two groups is as expected, with the poor showing lower price elasticity and higher income elasticity for staple foods; but the differences are not so great. On the other hand, no matter how food security is measured, it seems as if the "food insecure" simply do not prefer staple food: compared to the food secure, the food insecure have a relatively price elastic and income inelastic (the lowest among all groups) demand for staple food, despite lower availability or consumption levels.

Comparisons with other developing countries are hard to make, as published figures for farm family demand elasticities (profits variable) range all over the place, from negative to quite positive (*SSS*, 1986). The own-price elasticities for rice estimated by Strauss (1986) for Sierra Leone in the most comparable study are similar in signs and magnitudes, but his findings over low-to-high income ranges differ: they indicate that both the own-price elasticities (profits constant) and the profit effects are extremely high for lowest income groups, but fall sharply with income, so that the own-price elasticities (profits variable) are virtually unchanged across income groups. In China, the variation of behaviour over income groups is not so extreme, and the own-price elasticity (profits variable) actually changes from positive (backwards-bending supply curve) to quite negative as incomes increase.

Feed Demand Function

The estimated coefficients are listed in Table 5.7a-b. For what is supposed to be a set of stable technical relationships, the overall R^2s are low and highly variable (though all F-statistics are highly significant), and the estimated coefficients vary considerably. The derivatives of feed with respect to various livestock products should be estimates of feed conversion rates. Unfortunately, these derivatives are too low to be plausible: household production survey data on pig raising, for example, suggests that average feed conversion rates (which should be

below marginal rates, due to use of large amounts of green forage) are about 4.5 :
1 (feed to pork) or around two-to-one (feed to finished pigs), whereas our equations
produce estimates only a fraction of these. The estimates for poultry and eggs for
some groups are more plausible (3-4:1), as also for draft animals (150-200 kgs/year
per draft animal). The best explanation is that our model is misspecified, especially
for hogs -- which are fattened for 250-300 days, and most frequently sold near
Chinese New Years (i.e., in January-February), so that this year's production would
be based on last year's feed supply. Also it is likely that availability of surplus grain
determines livestock raising, whereas our model suggests that production determines
grain (requirements). However, absence of data on previous year's grain production,
feed grain set-asides, or year-end stocks makes it impossible to develop a more
appropriate model.

The model does produce price coefficients mostly of the right sign (a
positive relationship between the pork/feed price ratio and feed consumption),
although the top quintile and all "food insecure" groups are an exception which
cannot be explained. Similarly, derived own-price elasticities of demand for feed
grain (shown below in Table 5.9a-b) are mostly negative and small, at -0.03 on
average and -0.16 for the highest group. The elasticity of feed demand with respect
to the price of pork (one of the non-staple foods) is of the opposite sign and about
the same range of magnitudes.

Table 5.7a <u>Feed Equation: Parameter Estimates by Income Quintile</u>

| | Total | Income Quintile | | | | |
		I	II	III	IV	V
Intercept	501.708	247.079	304.661	575.478	560.541	1112.258
	(11.73)	(3.66)	(3.70)	(6.66)	(5.68)	(9.16)
Hogs	1.285	71.930	32.465	-0.111	60.776	1.249
	(1.85)	(3.27)	(1.66)	(0.05)	(3.43)	(1.103)
Pork	0.635	0.637	0.579	0.703	0.500	0.104
	(11.90)	(2.47)	(4.34)	(3.83)	(2.21)	(0.56)
Draft Animals	348.699	241.805	46.828	246.985	-268.028	1439.279
	(6.67)	(1.49)	(0.35)	(2.654)	(1.82)	(5.39)
Poultry	3.981	-0.223	9.622	-11.326	4.356	3.741
	(8.63)	(0.10)	(4.49)	(5.59)	(2.19)	(4.72)
Eggs	3.061	2.818	4.489	4.810	01.539	-0.101
	(42.46)	(5.49)	(6.43)	(8.94)	(2.98)	(0.50)
Hogs^2	-8.9e-04	-0.141	-0.082	2.1e-03	-0.270	-8.8e-03
	(2.65)	(3.35)	(1.66)	(0.13)	(3.21)	(1.46)
Pork^2	-1.6e-05	-3.8e-04	-1.4e-04	1.3e-03	-5.2e-04	7.9e-04
	(9.36)	(0.09)	(3.77)	(0.80)	(0.24)	(0.84)
Draft Animals^2	-15.309	-90.815	10.379	-11.014	292.483	-457.637
	(4.36)	(1.05)	(0.65)	(2.27)	(7.32)	(4.10)
Poultry^2	-3.8e-03	0.005	-0.014	0.121	-0.009	-0.003
	(13.88)	(0.43)	(4.01)	(13.45)	(2.11)	(7.61)
Eggs^2	-5.4e-05	0.002	-7.8e-03	-0.002	-9.3e-05	4.2e-03
	(40.79)	(6.31)	(0.80)	(5.65)	(2.88)	(16.35)
Pork/Feed Price	3.995	5.319	5.772	4.670	12.978	-12.966
	(1.62)	(1.31)	(1.19)	(1.04)	(2.81)	(1.82)
Region 1 Dummy	-103.660	56.772	84.045	-212.211	-565.167	-221.590
	(1.22)	(0.20)	(0.29)	(0.80)	(2.46)	(1.75)
Region 2	197.114	383.817	291.643	160.210	36.810	114.160
	(4.87)	(3.88)	(3.10)	(1.96)	(0.442)	(1.39)
Region 4	55.388	161.128	162.533	124.648	97.955	8.819
	(1.93)	(3.52)	(3.18)	(2.36)	(1.63)	(0.10)
Region 5	-67.966	54.268	34.130	-168.311	129.779	-86.565
	(1.22)	(0.80)	(0.378)	(1.45)	(0.93)	(0.38)
Plains	152.052	170.583	157.428	20.926	149.232	48.715
	(4.54)	(3.47)	(2.59)		(1.96)	(0.50)
Hilly	56.576	45.861	5.85	-69.856	10.958	-21.800
	(1.66)	(1.03)	(0.10)		(0.14)	(0.21)

Table 5.7b <u>Feed Equation: Parameter Estimates by Different Groups</u>

	County Status		Food Self-Sufficiency		Food Adequacy		Doubly
	Poor	Non-poor	Sufficient	Insufficient	Adequate	Inadequate	Insecure
Intercept	174.822	611.282	531.667	658.628	409.679	543.773	418.974
	(2.38)	(10.87)	(9.85)	(10.54)	(5.01)	(11.68)	(5.77)
Hogs	7.912	1.409	2.194	-1.405	1.363	16.164	41.396
	(1.45)	(1.61)	(2.62)	(0.91)	(1.48)	(3.23)	(1.93)
Pork	1.021	0.558	0.679	0.439	0.628	0.896	0.634
	(11.55)	(5.77)	(11.00)	(2.84)	(7.03)	(7.71)	(3.44)
Draft Animals	104.376	380.150	373.591	354.413	425.131	251.539	451.901
	(1.33)	(4.82)	(5.68)	(4.08)	(4.65)	(3.55)	(4.14)
Poultry	1.879	4.332	5.426	-2.277	4.980	0.492	-2.327
	(1.01)	(8.60)	(10.70)	(1.55)	(4.68)	(0.84)	(1.42)
Eggs	5.219	3.172	1.824	1.016	3.074	3.594	9.949
	(8.62)	(40.93)	(19.17)	(3.52)	(30.99)	(13.51)	(10.57)
Hogs^2	-2.0e-02	-8.5e-04	-1.3e-03	7.1e-04	-9.3e-04	-2.9e-02	-6.6e-02
	(1.75)	(1.76)	(3.35)	(0.67)	(2.12)	(3.29)	(1.95)
Pork^2	-2.6e-05	-3.5e-05	-1.7e-05	8.9e-05	-1.6e-05	-4.1e-04	-3.0e-04
	(10.51)	(0.52)	(8.99)	(0.68)	(5.86)	(3.53)	(1.76)
Draft Animals^2	-4.410	-6.322	-16.562	-20.417	-18.897	-13.102	-31.623
	(1.07)	(0.45)	(4.18)	(1.62)	(3.60)	(1.13)	(2.24)
Poultry^2	-4.5e-03	-4.0e-03	-3.7e-03	5.6e-03	-3.4e-03	-5.4e-04	5.8e-03
	(1.16)	(13.67)	(12.90)	(2.06)	(3.06)	(1.09)	(2.00)
Eggs^2	-2.6e-03	-5.6e-05	-3.2e-05	3.3e-04	-5.4e-05	-5.6e-04	-1.9e-02
	(7.94)	(39.42)	(18.72)	(10.82)	(30.05)	(5.40)	(5.43)
Pork/Feed Price	0.348	5.079	9.797	-7.810	11.764	-1.793	-4.064
	(0.08)	(1.79)	(3.42)	(1.96)	(2.54)	(0.69)	(0.87)
Region 1 Dummy	-468.658	-39.101	-11.682	-282.559	-208.505	-79.345	-156.338
	(2.27)	(0.42)	(0.10)	(2.76)	(1.50)	(0.76)	(1.12)
Region 2	380.889	177.203	97.450	473.416	235.535	156.842	436.915
	(3.56)	(3.97)	(1.94)	(8.26)	(2.95)	(3.77)	(6.83)
Region 4	250.860	30.549	108.149	-54.246	199.260	-42.555	-74.098
	(4.64)	(0.90)	(3.18)	(1.20)	(3.64)	(1.41)	(1.48)
Region 5	133.587	-32.974	-10.059	-146.120	55.340	-235.220	-218.867
	(1.81)	(0.42)	(0.15)	(1.87)	(0.58)	(3.62)	(2.26)
Plains	34.344	60.499	172.440	11.168	238.038	111.048	-33.622
	(0.52)	(1.32)	(3.95)		(3.74)	(3.13)	(0.64)
Hilly	145.304	-38.723	34.647	0.953	46.632	60.045	-11.369
	(3.20)	(0.81)	(0.78)		(0.74)	(1.65)	(0.22)

Derivation of Marketed Surplus Elasticities

The marketed surplus is calculated as the difference between production and human and livestock consumption of staple food (grain). Table 5.8a-b indicates the average values of these variables, as predicted from our equations, and the corresponding commercialization rate for staple food. On average, all households are net sellers, with an average net marketing rate of 27.5%. The rate is lowest (around 15%) for the lowest income quintile, residents in the poor counties, and for those not self-sufficient in foodgrains. All these groups have low per capita production (310-360 kgs/capita/year) and consumption (190-240 kgs/capita/year). The marketing rate jumps to 28% for the second lowest quintile and rises to 40% for the highest quintile as expected. Interestingly, the group with "adequate" food consumption only sells 8% of their production, whereas the consumption "inadequate" group has a rate equal to that of the highest quintile (39%), and even the "doubly insecure" group has a rate near 30%. Again, we do not consider that the low food consumers are really food insecure, but rather are just not "grain lovers".

Table 5.8a <u>Predicted Value of Income, Production and Feed by Income Quintile</u>

	Total	I	II	III	IV	V
		------------	Income Quintile	------------		
Predicted:						
Income pc (Y)	568	241	385	509	666	1,150
Production (jin)/1	4,777	3,422	4,662	5,234	5,282	5,591
Feed (jin)	949	569	684	745	806	837
Consumption (jin)	2,512	2,326	2,697	2,898	2,752	2,542
Market Surplus (jin)	1,316	527	1,282	1,591	1,723	2,211
Marketing %	27.5%	15.4%	27.5%	30.4%	32.6%	39.5%
% Expend. Grain	34.6%	69.3%	50.8%	42.5%	34.7%	20.2%
Grain Prod pc (kg)	471	309	434	513	541	623
Grain Cons pc (kg)	248	210	251	284	282	283

/1 Production (and consequently Marketed Surplus) is understated due to biases when prediction is made at the arithmetic means of exogenous variables, as opposed to geometric means (at which log-linear production functions are most accurate)

Table 5.8b <u>Predicted Value of Income, Production and Feed by Different Groups</u>

	County Status		Food Self-sufficiency		Consumption Adequacy		Doubly
	Poor	Non-poor	Sufficient	Insufficient	Adequate	Inadequate	Insecure
Predicted:							
Income pc (Y)	405	611	594	517	619	534	494
Production (jin)/1	3,842	5,216	5,748	3,280	4,947	4,567	3,447
Feed (jin)	772	996	1,038	755	1,103	842	717
Consumption (jin)	2,555	2,598	2,845	2,031	3,447	1,937	1,735
Market Surplus (jin)	515	1,622	1,865	494	398	1,788	994
Marketing %	13.4%	31.1%	32.4%	15.1%	8.0%	39.2%	28.8%
% Expend. Grain	47.2%	33.7%	38.2%	29.8%	44.2%	28.2%	26.7%
Grain Prod pc (kg)	363	519	577	311	514	433	319
Grain Cons pc (kg)	241	259	286	193	358	184	161

Estimated marketed surplus elasticities for staple food may be derived from the definition of marketed surplus as a weighted difference between the price elasticity of supply and the (profits variable) price elasticity of human consumption and price elasticity of feed consumption (Strauss, 1986), that is:

$$\frac{P_j}{|MS_i|}\frac{\partial MS_i}{\partial P_j} = \frac{Q_i}{|MS_i|}\frac{P_j}{Q_i}\frac{\partial Q_i}{\partial P_j} - \frac{C_i}{|MS_i|C_i}\frac{P_j}{\partial P_j}\frac{\partial C_i}{\partial P_j} - \frac{F_i}{|MS_i|}\frac{P_j}{F_i}\frac{\partial F_i}{\partial P_j} \text{ where } |MS_i| \text{ is}$$

the absolute value of the marketed surplus of grain, Q_i is total output of grain, C_i is consumption of grain, and F_i is grain for feed, and the P_js represent the prices of staple, non-staple, and other food .

Price elasticities of marketed surplus are presented in Table 5.9a-b. All but one (second bottom income quintile) of the own-price elasticities of marketed surplus are positive, although the elasticities for the lowest two income groups prove zero or negative, due to positive price elasticities of consumption elasticities (profits variable) and fairly high income elasticities of demand. Compared to Strauss' finding in Sierra Leone, where marketed surplus elasticities for rice are relatively uniform over income groups, our data indicates that the elasticities rise sharply with increased incomes. On average, the elasticity is almost unity (0.91), but there are major differences among groups. Marketed surplus is very price elastic in the poor areas (1.76), mainly because the base (14%) is so low, but also because (in comparison to the poor in income) the residents of poor counties have somewhat higher price elasticity of consumption and somewhat lower one with profit effect than the non-poor areas. The various "food insecure" groups show inconsistent market surplus elasticities. The "food insufficient" group has a quite high elasticity (2.53), followed by the "double insecure", who have above-unity elasticity. The "food inadequate" group is price inelastic of marketed surplus (0.66), perhaps because the current marketed surplus rate is very high. The highest elasticity is that of the "adequate food consumption" group -- the "grain lovers", whose existing marketing rate is extraordinarily low (8%). Not too much should be made of the largest elasticities, since in all these cases the high numbers are due to the low current level of marketed surplus (relative to production and consumption). The more important observation is that market surplus elasticities are positive and substantial for all groupings but the two lowest quintiles in income. It is noticed that the "food insufficient" group has low production yet is willing to sell more in response to price increase, while "food inadequate" group has sufficient production, but is unwilling to sell more. The "food insufficient" appear to be engaged mainly in production of non-staples or non-farm activities, to depend heavily on purchased food, and therefore to be exceptionally responsive to market prices. The "food inadequate" may be pressed (by sales quota or income needs) to sell more than they would normally prefer; or tend to be at "corner solutions" rather than "internal solutions", and so respond weakly to price incentives.

Market surplus elasticities increase substantially across income quintiles, reaching 0.66 for the highest quintile. This is because both elasticities of supply and demand increase with income. The bottom two quintiles have insignificant or even negative elasticities of market supply (backwards-bending marketed supply curve). This is due largely to the profit effect: because the incomes of the poor depend so heavily on grain production, and the income elasticities of foodgrain demand are so high, increased market price leads to increased own consumption and even decreased marketing.

It is also possible to estimate cross-price elasticities of marketed surplus of grain with respect to non-staple food, taking advantage of the fact that the prices of pork, vegetables and oilseed are included in the supply function and the price of pork in the feed demand function (the assumption is made that all of these increase in the same proportion as the overall price index for non-staple foods). The profit effect is much smaller for non-staple foods (which account for a smaller proportion of family income), and reinforces the positive cross-price demand elasticities. As a result, the cross-price elasticities of market surplus of staple foods with respect to non-staple foods are large and negative in sign -- that is, increases in the price of cash crops which compete with grain (e.g., vegetables and oilseeds) cause reduced production and increased consumption of grain, and simultaneous increases in pork prices induce increased feed use in livestock raising, so that the overall effect is a very strong contraction in marketed surplus. In this one case, the effect appears strongest for the poor in income, residents of poor counties, those not self-sufficient in food, and those doubly insecure -- groups whose response to grain price increases is not so uniform. However, those groups would reduce their marketed surplus of staple food considerably in response to an increase in cash crop prices and *vice versa*.

The estimation results for marketed surplus can also be used test the hypotheses about risk. As mentioned in the previous chapter, it is difficult to measure risk and attitude to risk. However, the risk model led to the conclusion that larger budget share of food would be associated with reduced marketing of food. This association is found in our data, which indicates that the relationships in China are at least consistent with the hypothesis from the risk model.

Table 5.9a <u>Price Elasticity of Marketed Surplus of Staple Food by Income Quintile</u>

Elasticity of:	with respect to:	Total	Income Quintile				
			I	II	III	IV	V
Market Surplus	Price of Grain	0.914	0.003	-0.255	0.384	0.6270	0.661
Production	"	0.019	0.008	-0.018	0.026	0.023	0.049
Feed	"	-0.033	-0.016	-0.025	-0.008	-0.155	0.117
Consumption	" (profit constant)	-0.760	-0.550	-0.621	-0.727	-0.767	-0.790
Consumption	" (profit variable)	-0.430	0.015	0.097	-0.162	-0.302	-0.506
Market Surplus	Price of Nonstaple	-1.069	-2.922	-0.912	-0.653	-0.749	-0.565
Production	"	-0.099	-0.166	-0.081	-0.053	-0.082	-0.102
Feed	"	0.025	0.011	0.018	0.006	0.110	-0.087
Consumption	" (profit constant)	0.346	0.386	0.252	0.236	0.257	0.276
Consumption	" (profit changing)	0.363	0.415	0.288	0.262	0.280	0.293
Consumption	Price of Nonstaple	0.086	0.233	0.046	0.047	0.053	0.054
Consumption	Income	0.049	0.550	0.832	0.717	0.683	0.610

/1 On the production side, the sum of the elasticities with respect to pork and vegetables are taken as representing the elasticity w.r.t. nonstaple food; similarly, in the feed equation, pork price appears, and the elasticity w.r.t. pork prices is taken as that w.r.t. non-staple foods (meat is a major component of nonstaple foods).

Table 5.9b <u>Price Elasticity of Marketed Surplus of Staple Food by Different Groups</u>

Elasticity of:	with respect to:	Country Status		Food Self-Sufficiency		Consumption Adequacy		Doubly
		Poor	Non-poor	Suffic ient	Insuff icient	Adequate	Inade quate	Insecure
Market Surplus	Price of Grain	1.756	0.714	0.624	2.527	3.887	0.660	1.153
Production	"	0.012	0.022	0.008	0.037	0.001	0.044	0.035
Feed	"	-0.004	-0.040	-0.074	0.086	-0.087	0.017	0.047
Consumption	" (profit constant)	-0.759	-0.713	-0.746	-0.808	-0.735	-0.804	-0.827
Consumption	" (profit changing)	-0.335	-0.387	-0.366	-0.586	-0.420	-0.513	-0.611
Market Surplus	Price of Nonstaples	-2.079	-0.870	-0.692	-2.780	-4.019	-0.732	-1.261
Production	"	-0.058	-0.093	-0.051	-0.158	-0.075	-0.106	-0.150
Feed	"	0.002	0.031	0.056	-0.063	0.066	-0.012	-0.033
Consumption	" (profit constant)	0.306	0.328	0.313	0.430	0.315	0.418	0.427
Consumption	" (profit changing)	0.332	0.344	0.331	0.444	0.335	0.431	0.439
Consumption	Price of Other Food	0.070	0.076	0.062	0.102	0.069	0.080	0.098
Consumption	Income	0.590	0.472	0.489	0.444	0.497	0.419	0.394

VI. CONCLUSIONS AND POLICY IMPLICATIONS

The estimated results in the previous section now can answer the questions raised in the beginning of this study: **with the growth of commercial production in China, will market forces largely solve the food security problems of the poor, or will special administrative measures need be taken to address food security problems? Can commercialization occur in poverty areas or among poor groups in China? Is Chinese rural poverty closely associated with food insecurity?** These results are also important to policy makers.

At present in rural China, there appears to be no serious food insecurity issue, despite substantial concern about this issue in the past. We sought to identify households with a measured food deficit, based on (a) lack of self-sufficiency (total food production less than 2,400 KCal per capita); (b) inadequate consumption (total food consumption less than 2,400 KCal per capita); and (c) "doubly insecure", that is both (a) and (b) or both insufficient production and consumption. These three groups accounted for 31, 57, and 25 percent of the (utilized portion of the) sample respectively. However, it turned out that all three groups had average incomes within the median quintile. Those who were not self-sufficient in food production on average purchased enough food to add nearly 50% to caloric intake, reaching a standard of about 2,000 KCal. Those whose food consumption appeared inadequate marketed on average almost 40% of their staple food production -- equivalent to the highest income quintile. As they did not buy much food, their consumption averaged a low 1,657 KCal (this is the *majority* of the sample!), however, their production was double their consumption (3,266 KCal). Even the "doubly insecure" had marketing rates of nearly 30% (roughly at the mean for the middle quintile), yet only 1,500 KCal per capita consumption.

Most remarkable, all three "food insecure" groups had income elasticities of staple food consumption <u>below</u> rather than above those of the other farm households. Finally, the measured "food insecure" are much more price-responsive in their consumption and marketing behaviour than, for example, households which are poor in income. There is no indication from the sample data that the food insecure households are forced by factors such as excessive quotas, debts, medical expenses, or taxes to market food which they would prefer to consume. Indeed, their voluntary marketing proportions (free market or negotiated sales) are higher on average than other households. Therefore, again it seems that these people are not seriously food insecure, and the low food consumption is not a constraint on marketing.

Since the household consumption data is not complete, it is likely that actual consumption somewhat <u>exceeds</u> our estimates. Also, it is likely that the official standard of food adequacy of 2,400 KCal *per capita* (not per adult equivalent) is *too* high. Nevertheless, the <u>measured</u> food insecure in general do not seem <u>constrained</u> to inadequate diets -- those who are not food self-sufficient may have chosen to specialize in cash crops, and those who consume low amounts of food may simply have low demands for grain (partly due to larger and younger households, and partly due to preference for other commodities).

In the officially-defined poor areas the average food consumption is over the official minimum requirements -- in fact, at levels above those of the lowest 60% of rural households. The residents in poor counties, thus, are not food insecure even by high official criterion. Of course, this may be partly due to subsidized food supply to the poor counties, but we saw earlier that subsidies to households, even in the poor areas, were only a small part of total cash and commodity income. The current marketed surplus in the poor counties is the lowest among all groups -- they consume more and sell less.

There are about 20% of sample households with an income below the poverty line (260 yuan). Their food consumption is 13% lower than the "minimum standard" of 2,400 KCal, but it is also higher that those in the three "food insecure" categories. In general this group has marginally sufficient grain production, and cannot be considered really food insecure.

We must conclude that the poor are not in general food insecure, and that food insecurity is no longer much of a problem in China. This is probably due to the fact that land distribution is extremely equal among income groups in rural China (although the quality of land is not) -- giving the poor a basis for meeting their food needs. In addition, the government's policy of relaxation of constraints on marketing and promotion of commercial production has encouraged the poor to expand their production.

However, the three "food insecure" groups do have low consumption levels compared with the average (conversely, the "food secure" seem to consume too many calories -- around 3,200 Kcal per day). It remains possible that estimated consumption levels are distorted due to errors in data entry -- for example, if consumption of processed grain were recorded in categories supposedly measured in units of unprocessed grain. Not enough is known about the distribution of caloric requirements about the mean or over a sample population to be sure when low consumption of energy reflects malnutrition. Further research is needed, with supplementary surveys, for example, to find out whether the low energy consumers are malnourished, especially for children (by using anthropomorphic indicators, e.g., weight-for-age, height-for-age); or whether such consumers are substituting nonstaple food (e.g., livestock products) not recorded in the sample survey for grain.

Having questioned the importance of the food security issue in China, we now need to focus only on the relationship between commercialization and poverty (low-income group and the official defined "poor counties). In most of the empirical work, we have treated commercialization as an endogenous outcome of household decisions. So to "promote" commercialization means to influence family decisions in such a way that they increase their cash sales and purchases. One way which government might try to influence decisions is through price policies.

The regression results suggested that staple food supply (production) elasticities with respect to market price were low across all groups. We attribute this to the fact that nearly one-half of households are at "corner solutions" where they make no voluntary sales of grain. This conclusion is somewhat surprising: in recent Chinese experience, grain production rose significantly to a peak in 1984 following official procurement price increases (but declines in free market prices) at the beginning of economic reform, and this has led many to conclude that the farmers' supply response was very positive. However, this was accompanied by a shift of land out of grain, as well as rapid growth of industrial input supply (especially chemical fertilizers) and introduction of new technology (e.g., hybrid rice and maize). Policy changes, such as relaxed control over farmers' cropping decisions and relaxation of restrictions on the free market, also confuse the picture of causation. Moreover, adverse price trends for grain relative to other crops occurred during the early 1980s, and trends in the real terms of trade of grain for industrial products such as fertilizer were negative in the late 1980s, both without causing major declines in grain production. Hence we regard the low own-price supply elasticities as plausible.

On the other hand, the *marketed* supply elasticities with respect to price were impressively high. This applies to both own-price and cross-price elasticities (with respect to non-staple food prices) of marketed surplus for staple foods, though with much variability across the various groups. The farmers resident in poor areas prove to have quite high price elasticities of marketed surplus. Although this is partly due to the very low current marketing rates, still it demonstrates that these farmers will respond to price incentives by increasing their commercialization rates.

This is not true for the poor in income, however: due to the heavy dependence of the rural poor on grain production as an income source and high income elasticity of demand for food, the two lowest quintiles have zero and negative own-price market surplus elasticities respectively. So at present the poor in income may not respond to overall price increases by becoming more commercialized.

But the government generally has no direct influence over market prices - - only over contract (quota) prices, accounting for under half of total sales of grain. We have seen that contract or quota prices should, in theory, have no influence on farmer's decisions about consumption or production, except through their influence on farm profits (profit effect). If the government attempts to promote commercialization by increasing quota prices, it is likely to backfire: this will increase farmers' income, causing them to consume more products (profit effect times high income elasticity of food consumption) and marketed surplus will decline. Dropping the contract (quota) system and unifying on market prices will have the same effect (unless it causes an overall shift in market prices).

This does not mean that the government should maintain fixed quota prices or should avoid eliminating the quota system! Rather, the government should choose a time at which the market surplus exceeds requirements in order to eliminate the quota system. This was the objective in 1985, but unfortunately the government lost its courage when the market surplus contracted in response, and effectively reimposed quotas.

There are two other policy approaches which would be more effective in increasing commercialization. The first is based on the observation that the income elasticity of demand for staple foods is surprisingly high, over all income groups, and that this contributes to the profit effect and reduces the market surplus elasticities.

One reason for such a high income elasticity may be a shortage of attractive consumer goods in the rural areas, especially consumer durables. If the consumer desires of farmers are aroused, the income elasticity of demand for food, especially staple food, should decline, and this will encourage marketing (and increase the market surplus price elasticity).

Second, the fundamental difference between the poor and the non-poor (whether based on incomes or area of residence) is found, not in commercial behaviour, but in productivity. This is seen clearly in the different intercepts and dummies in the production function estimates, as well as differences in land quality (irrigated percentage) and input levels between poor and non-poor. The economic behaviour of the poor seems "normal" -- there is no evidence of "subsistence first" behaviour, for example. Yet, because of low productivity per capita, the average marketing percentage for the poor is still very low. Since unfavorable natural resources and poor infrastructure are basic causes of low productivity, improvement of rural infrastructure and assistance in developing more advanced technologies would be the most critical parts of a poverty alleviation strategy. Improved productivity, leading to higher incomes, is certain to lead to higher levels of commercialization.

Overall, after a decade of the rural economic reform with a growth of productivity and commercialization, rural China's food security problem has been basically solved. It is no longer a major government policy issue, nor does the government need special policies or measures to deal with it. Currently poverty is the major policy concern, and promotion of commercialization is considered by government an effective approach to deal with poverty. However, as shown above, the poor in income are not likely to commercialize in response to improved price incentives, but may respond to more attractive or abundant consumer goods. The residents of poor areas, who may be responsive to incentives, are still constrained by low productivity to at most small market surpluses. Therefore, measures such as assistance in infrastructure investment are needed to help lift the poor areas out of poverty status.

REFERENCES

Adulavidhaya, Kamphol, Yoshimi Kuroda, Lawrence lau, and Pan Yotopoulos. 1984. "The Comparative Statics of the Behaviour of Agricultural Households in Thailand." *Singapore Economic Review*, 29: 67-96.

Adulavidhaya, Kamphol, Yoshimi Kuroda, Lawrence lau, Pichit Lerttamrab, and Pan Yotopoulos. 1979. "A Microeconomic Analysis of the Agriculture of Thailand." *Food Research Studies*, 17: 79-86.

Ahmad, Ehtisham and Athar Hussain. 1991. *Social Security in China: A Historical Perspective*. In Social Security in Developing Countries eds. by Ehtisham Ahmad, Jean Dreze, John Hills and Amartya Sen. Oxford, U.K.: Clarendon Press. New York: Oxford university press.

Ahmed, Raisuddin. 1989. *Investment in Rural Infrastructure: Criical Role for Commercialization*. Paper contributed to the Policy Workshop of the IFPRI. Washington, D.C.: International Food POlicy Researcy Institute.

Bardhan, Kalpana. 1970. Price and Output Response of Marketed Surplus of Foodgrains: A Cross-Sectional Study of Some North Indian Villages. American Journal of Agricultural Economics. vol. 52. no. 1.

Barnett, A. Doak. China and the World Food System. 1979. Overseas Development Council.

Barnum, Howard, and Lyn Squire. 1978. "Thechnology and Relative Economic Efficiency." *Oxford Economic Papers*, 30: 181-98.

_____. 1979a. "An Econometric Application of the Theory of the Farm Household." *Journal of Development Economics*, 6: 79-102.

_____. 1979b. A model of an Agricultural Household. Washington, D.C.: The World Bank.

Beaton, G., A. Kelly, J. Kevany, R. Martorell, and J. Mason. 1991. Appropriate Uses of Anthropometric Indicators in Children. Nutrition Polucy Discussion Paper 7. Geneva: United Nations Administritive Committee on Coordination -- Subcommittee on Nutrition.

Becker, G. S. 1965. "A Theory of the Allocation of Times." *Economic Journal*, 75: 493-517.

_____. 1981. A Treatise on the Family. Cambridge, MASS: Harvard University Press.

Behrman, Jere R. 1966. Price Elasticity of the Marketed Surplus of a Subsistence Crop. Journal of Farm Economics. vol. 48. no. 4 part I.

Berry, Sara S. 1984. *Households, Decision Making, and Rural Development: Do We Need to Know More?* Development Discussion Paper 167. Harvard Institute for International Development.

Binswanger, Hans, and Mark Rosenzweig, eds. 1984. Contractual Arrangements, Employment, and Wages in Rural Labor Markets in Asia. Hew haven, Conn.: Yale University Press.

Bouis, Howarth E, and lawrence J. Haddad. 1990. *Effect of Agricultural Commercialization on Land Tenure, Household Resource Allocation, and Nutrition in the Philippines.* Research Report 79. Washington, D.C.: International Food Policy Research Institute.

_____. 1992. Are Estimation of Calorie-income Elasticities too High? A Recalibration of the Plausible Range. *Journal of Development Economics,* 39: 333-364.

von Braun, Joachim. 1989. Commercialization in Developing Countries. Paper submitted to the Conference of Agricultural Commercialization in Developing countries.

von Braun, Joachim, Hartwig de Haen, and Juergen Blanken. 1991. *Commercialization of Agriculture under Population Pressure: Effects on Production, Consumption, and Nutrition in Rwanda.* Research Report 85. Washington, D.C.: International Food Policy Research Institute.

von Braun, Joachim, Howarth Bouis, Shubh Kumar, and Rajul Pandya-Lorch. 1992. *Improving Food Security of the Poor. Concept, Policy, and Programs.* Washington, D.C.: International Food Policy Research Institute.

von Braun, Joachim, David Hotchkiss and Maarten Immink. 1989. *Nontraditional Export Crops in Guatemala: Effects on Production, Income, and Nutrition.* Research Report 73. Washington, D.C.: International Food Policy Research Institute.

von Braun, Joachim and Eileen T. Kennedy. 1986. *Commercialization of subsistence agriculture : Income and Nutritional Effects in Developing Counties.* Working Paper on Commercialization of Agriculture and Nutrition. no. 1. Washington, D.C.: International Food Policy Research Institute.

von Braun, Joachim and Rajur Pandya-Lorch eds. 1991. *Income Sources of Malnourished People in Rural Areas: Microlevel Information and Policy Implications*. Working Papers on Commercialization on Agriculture and nutrition. no. 5. Washington, D.C.: International Food Policy Research Institute.

von Braun, Joachim, Detlev Puetz, and Patrick Webb. 1989. *Irrigation Technology and Commercialization of Rice in the Gambia: Effects on Income and Nutrition*. Research Report 75. Washington, D.C.: International Food Policy Research Institute.

Bridge, J. I. 1971. Applied Econometrics. North Holland Publishing Co. Netherlands.

Broca, Sumiter and Peter Oram. 1991. Study on the Location of the Poor. Memo. Washington, D.C.: International Food Policy Research Institute.

Bryceson, Deborah F. 1988. Peasant Cash Cropping versus Self-Sufficiency in Tanzania: A historical Perspective. IDS Bulletin. vol. 19. no. 2.

Chayanov, A. V. 1925. The Theory of Peasant Economy. Moscow: Cooperative Publishing House. eds. by D. Thornor, B, Kerblay, and R. E. F. Smith. Homewood,. III.: Richard Irwin, 1966.

Chinese Agricultural Yearbook Edition Committee (CAYEC). 1983-1990. Zhongguo Nongye Nianjian (Chinese Agricultural Yearbook). Beijing: Agricultural Publishing House.

Cohen, Ronald. 1988. Introduction: Guidance and Misguidance in Africa's Food Production. in Satisfying Africa's Food Needs: Food Production and Commercialization in African Agriculture. ed by Ronald Cohen. Lynnef Rienner Publishers. Boulder/london.

Crook. Frederick W. 1988. China's Grain Supply and Use Balance Sheets. in Agriculture and Trade Report. *Situation and Outlook Series*. USDA ERS. June 1988.

_____. 1991. China's Eighth Five Year Plan: Goals and Target for the Agricultural Sector (Part I and II). *CPE Agriculture Report*. vol. IV no. 6. USDA ERS.

Dhrymes, Phoebus J. 1978. Introductory Econometrics. Springer-Verlag.

Division of Agricultural Statistics of State Statistics Bureau of China (DASSSB). 1984. Zhongguo Nongye de Guanghui Chengjiu (The Splendid Achievement of China's Agriculture). 1949--1984. Chinese Statistics Publishing House.

_____. 1985-1992. Zhongguo Nongcun Tongji Nianjian (Chinese Rural Statistics Yearbook). Beijing: Chinese Statistics Publishing House.

Division of Trade and Price of SSB (DTPSSB). 1984. Zhongguo Maoyi Wujia Tongji Ziliao (Chinese Trade and Price Statistics Data). 1952-1983. Beijing: Chinese Statistics Publishing House.

Dreze, Jean, and Amartya Sen. 1989. Hunger and Public Action. Oxford: Clarendon Press.

Edirisinghe, Neville. 1987. *The Food Stamps Scheme in Sri Lanka: Costs, Benefits, and Options for Modification.* Research Report 58. Washington, D.C.: International Food Policy Research Institute.

Ellis, Frank. 1988, Cash Cropsand Distribution: Small-Farm Sugar Production in Fiji: Employment and Distribution Aspects. IDS Bulletin. vol. 19. no. 2.

Epstein, L. 1975. A Disaggregate Analysis of Consumer Choice under Uncertainty. *Econometrica*, 43: 877-892.

Ezekiel, Hannan and Johann C. Stuyt. 1989. The Maharashtra Employment Guarantee Scheme: Its Response to Differences in Employment Patterns Between Districts. *The Economic Times* (Bombay), May 31- June 2.

Fafchamps, Marcel. 1992. Cash Crop Production, Food Price Volatility, and Rural Market Integration in the Third World. *American Journal of Agricultural Economics*, 1992, 74: 90-99.

Feder, Gershon, Lawrence J. Lau, Justin Y. Lin and Xiaopeng Luo. 1990. *The Determinants of Farm Investment and Residential Construction in Post-Reform China.* World Bank working paper WPS 471. Washington, D.C.: The World Bank.

_____.1991.*Credit'sEffectonProductivity in Chinese Agriculture A Microeconomic Model of Disequilibrium.* World Bank working paper WPS 571. Washington, D.C.: The World Bank.

Finkelshtain, Israel and James A. Chalfant. 1991. "Marketed Surplus Under Risk: Do Peasants Agree with Sandmo?" *American Journal of Agricultural Economics*, 1991, 73: 557-567.

Folbre, Nancy. 1986. Cleaning House: New Perspectives on Households and Economic Development. Journal of Development Economics. vol. 22. no. 1.

Gao, Hongbin et al. 1991. An Alternative Between Survival and Development. Case Study of Anti-Poverty. Beijing: Chinese Development Publishing House.

Gao, Xiaomeng. 1987. The Memorandum of Grain Problem. in Research of China's Grain Problem eds by Gao Xiaomeng and Song Guoqing and others. Bejing: Economic management publishing House. Beijing.

_____. 1989a. The Current Situation and Reform of Chinese Grain Procurement System. *Development Research Dispatch*, no. 12. Development Research Institute of State Council.

_____. 1989b. Over-Normal Increase and Over-Normal Delay -- Recovery and Disappearance of Farm household Food Security. *Development Research Dispatch*, no. 13. Development Research Institute of State Council.

General Survey Team of Rural Economy of SSB (GSTSSB). 1988. 1990. Zhongguo Fenxian Tongji Ziliao (Chinese County Statistics Data). Beijing: Chinese Statistics Publishing House.

Gittinger, J. Price, J. Leslie, C. Hoisington. 1987. Food Policy Integrating Supply, Distribution, and Consumption. EDI series in Economic Development.

Groen, H. and J. Kilpatrick. 1978. China's Agricultural Production in Chinese Economy Post-Mao.

Guizhou Sheng Jiaotong Ting (Guizhou Transportation Bureau, Guizhou). 1989. Gonglu Jiaotong yu Jingji Kafa (Road Construction and Economic Development).

Haessel, Walter. 1975. The Price and Income Elasticities of Home Consumption and Marketed Surplus of Foodgrains. American Journal of Agricultural Economics. vol. 57. no. 1.

Haddad, Lawrence J., Joan Sullivan, and Eileen Kennedy. 1991. identification and Evaluation of Alternative Indicators of Food and Nutrition Security: Some Conceptual Issues and an Analysis of Extant Data. International Food Policy Research Institute, Washington, D.C. Mimeo.

Hammer, Jeffrey S. 1986. "Subsistence First' Farm allocation decisions in Senegal. *Journal of Development Economics*, 23: 355-69.

Hazell, Peter B.R. 1982. Aplication of Risk Preference Estimates in Firm-Household and Agricultural Sector Models. *American Journal of Agricultural Economics*, 64(2): 384-90.

Hazell, Peter B. R., R.D. Norton, M. Parthasarathy, C. Pomareda. 1983. The Importance of Risk in Agricultural Planning Models. CHAC: Programming Studies for Mexican Agriculture. Baltimore, MD: The John Hopkins University Press.

Hazell, Peter B. R., P.L. Scandizzo. 1983. Risk in Market Equilibrium Models for Agriculture. CHAC: Programming Studies for Mexican Agriculture. Baltimore, MD: The John Hopkins University Press.

Heckman, James, and Thomas E. MaCurdy. 1981. *New Methods for Estimating Labor Supply Functions: A Survey*. In Research in Labor Economics vol. 4. ed. by Roland G. Ehrenberg.

Hinderink, J. and M. Sterkenburg. 1987. Agricultural Commercialization and Government Policy in Africa. london: KPI Limited.

Jiang, Dehua, Zhang Yaoguang, Yang Liu, and Hou Shaofan. 1989. The Type and Development of China's Poor Areas. Beijing: Tourism Education Publishing House.

Jiang, Zhongyi. 1990. The Standard and Measurement of China's Poverty. Unpublished memo.

Jones, Christine and Michael Roemer. 1991. *The Behaviour of Parallel Markets In Developing Countries*. in Markets in Developing Countries. in Parallel, Fragmented, and Black. ed. by C. Jones and M. Roemer. International Centre for Economic Growth. Harvard Institute for International Development.

Kennedy, Eileen T. and Bruce Cogill. 1987. *Income and Nutritional Effects of the Commercialization of Agriculture in Southwestern Kenya.* Research Report 79. Washington, D.C.: International Food Policy Research Institute.

Kennedy, Eileen T. and Harold H. Alderman. 1987. *Comparative Analyses of Nutritional Effectiveness of Food Subsidies and Other Food-Related Interventions*. Joint WHO-UNICEF Nutrition Support Programme.   Washington, D.C.: International Food Policy Research Institute.

Khan, Azizur Rahman, Keith Griffin, Carl Riskin, and Zhao Renwei. 1992. *Household Income and Its Distribution in China*. Working paper 92-3 in economics. Department of Economics, University of California Riverside.

Khan, Azizur Rahman. 1992. *Determinants of Household Income in Rural China*. Working paper 92-9 in economics. Department of Economics, University of California Riverside.

Kmenta, Jan. 1986. Elements of Econometrics. Second edition. Macmillan Publishing Company. New York: Collier Macmillan Publishers.

Konandreas, Panos, B. Huddleston, V. Ramangkura. 1978. *Food Security: an Insurance Approach*. Research Report 4. Washington, D.C.: International Food Policy Research Institute.

Kumar, Shubh K. and Omar Haider Chowdhury. 1985. The Effects on Nutritional Status. In Development Impact of the Food-for-Work Program in Bangladesh, BIDS/IFPRI. Submitted to the World Food Programme. Washington, D.C.: International Food Policy Research Institute.

Kuroda, Yoshimi, and Pan Yotopolous. 1978. A Microeconomic Analysis of Production Behaviour of the Farm Household in Japan: A Profit Function Approach. *The Economic Review (Japan)*, 29: 116-29.

_____. 1980. A Study of Consumption Behaviour of the Farm Household in Japan: An Application of the Linear Logarithmic Expenditure System. *The Economic Review (Japan)*, 31: 1-15.

Lardy, Nicholas R. 1982. *Food Consumption in the People's Republic of China*. in The Chinese Agricultural Economy. ed. by R. Baker, R. Sinha and B. Rose. Westview Press Inc.

_____. 1983. Agriculture in China's Modern Economic Development. Cambridge: Cambridge University Press.

Lau, lawrence, Wuu-long Lin, and Pan Yotopoulos. 1978. The Linear Logarithmic Expenditure System: An Application to Consumption Leisure Choice. *Econometrica*, 46: 843-68.

Lele, Uma. 1987. Structural Adjustment, Agricultural Development and the Poor: Some Observations on Malawi. Mimeo. World Bank, Washington, D.C.

Leonard, H. Jeffrey, and Contributors. 1989. Environment and the Poor: Development Strategies for a Common Agenda. U.S.-Third World Policy Perspectives 11. New Brunswick, N.J.: Transaction Books.

Lipton, Michael. 1968. The Theory of The 'Optimising Peasant'. *Journal of Development Studies*, 4(3)327-51.

Malinvaud, E. 1969. First Order Certainty Equivalence. *Econometrica*. 37: 706-718.

Matthews, Alan. 1988. Cash Crops and Grows: Growth and Employment Consideration in the Food vs. Export Crops Debate. IDS Bulletin. vol. 19. no. 2.

Maxwell, Simon and Adrian Fernando. 1989. Cash Crop in Developing Countries: The Issues, The Facts, The policies. World Development. vol. 17, no. 11.

Maxwell, Simon. 1988. Editorial. IDS Bulletin. vol. 19. no. 2.

Maxwell, S. J. and H.W. Singer. 1979. Food Aid to Developing Countries: A Survey. World Development. vol. 7. no.3.

Nakajima, Chihiro. 1969. *Subsistence and Commercial Family Farms: Some Theoretical Models of Subjective Equilibrium*. in Subsistence Agriculture and Economic Development. ed. by Clifton R, Wharton, Jr. Chicago: Aldine.

Newbery, David M. G. and Joseph E. Stiglitz. 1981. The Theory of Commodity Price Stabilization A Study in the Economics of Risk. Clarendon Press. Oxford.

Office of the Leading Group of Economic Development in Poor Areas Under State Council (OLGEDPA). 1989. Outline of Economic Development in China's Poor Areas. Bejing: Chinese Agricultural Publishing House.

Oi, Jean C. 1989. State and Peasants in Contemporary China. The Political Economy of Village Government. University of California Press.

Parish, William L. 1985. *Introduction: Historical Background and Current Issues*. in Chinese Rural Development The Great Transformation. ed. by W.L. Parish M.E. Sharpe, Inc.

Perkins, Dwight H. 1966. Market Control and Planning in Communist China. Cambridge, Massachusetts: Harvard University Press.

Piazza, Alan. 1986. Food Consumption and Nutritional Status in the PRC. Westview Special Studies on China. Westview Press.

Pitt, Mark M. and Mark R. Rosenzweig. 1986. *Agricultural Prices, Food Consumption, and the Health and Productivity of Indonesian Farmers*. In Agricultural Household Model. eds. by Singh, Inderjit, Lyn Squire, and John Strauss. Baltimore, MD: The John Hopkins University Press.

Pratt, John W. 1964. Risk Aversion in the Small and in the Large. *Econometrica*, 32: 122-140.

Pinstrup-Andersen, Per and M. Garcia. 1983. *Data on Food Consumption by High-Risk Family Members: Its Utility for Identifying Target Household for Food and Nutrition Programmes*. Workshop on Measuring Intra-household Resource Allocation.

Pinstrup-Andersen, Per. 1988. *The Social and Economic Effects of Consumer-Oriented Subsidies: A Summary of Current Evidence*. In Food Subsidies in Developing Countries: Costs, Benefits, and Policy Options. ed. by Per Pinstrup-Andersen. Baltimore MD.: The John Hopkins University Press.

Pinstrup-Andersen, Per and Harold Alderman. 1988. *The Effectiveness of Consumer-Oriented Food Subsidies in Reaching Rationing and Income Transfer Goals*. In Food Subsidies in Developing Countries: Costs, Benefits, and Policy Options. ed. by Per Pinstrup-Andersen. Baltimore MD.: The John Hopkins University Press.

Randolph, Thomas Fitz. 1992. The impact of Agricultural Commercialization on Child Nutrition: A Case Study of Smallholder Households in Malawi. Unpublished Ph.D. dissertation. Cornell University.

RAWOO. 1986. Food Security in Developing Countries Research Needs and Conditions. General Recommendations 4.

Readon, Thomas, P. Matlon and C. Delgado. 1988. Coping with Household-level Food Insecurity in Drought-affected Areas of Bukina Faso. *World Development*, 16 (9): 1065-74.

Research Group of "Commodity Circulation in Rural Areas" (RGCCRA). 1989. Comprehensive Research Report of the Marketing of Agricultural Products in Rural China during 1986-2000.

Research Group of China's Rural Development Issues (RGCRDI). 1984. The Systematical Survey of Rural Economic Reform. Bejing: Chinese Socialist Sciences Press.

Research Group of China's Poor Areas of SSB (RGCPA). 1990. Regional Distribution of Poor Population, Poor Households and Poor regions in Rural China. Research Report no. 2.

Research Group of China's Rural Areas of SSB (RGCPA). 1989. Research Report of the Poverty Cretirion of China's Rural Areas. Research Report no.1.

Research Group of China's Rural Development Issues (RGCRDI). 1984. The Systematic Survey of Rural Economic Reform. Beijing: Chinese Social Sciences Publishing House.

Research Institute of Rural Development, Chinese Academy of Social Sciences (RIRDCASS). 1991. The Effect of the Quality of Grassroots Cadres in Poor Regions to the Economic Development. Research Report. (cited from Zhu Ling. 1992)

Renlow, Mitch. 1990. "Household Inventories and Marketed Surplus in Semisubsistence Agriculture." *American Journal of Agricultural Economics*, 24. 72 (3): 664-75.

Reutlinger, Shlomo. 1987. *Food Security and Poverty in Developing Countries*. in Food Policy. edited. by J. P. Gittinger et al. EDI. Series in Economic Development. Baltimore. MD.: The John Hopkins University Press.

Roemer, Michael and Christine Jones. 1991. Markets in Developing Countries Parallel, Fragmented, and Black. International Centre for Economic Growth & Harvard Institute for International Development. San Francisco: ICS Press.

Roumasset, James A. 1980. Rice and Risk. Amsterdam: North Holland.

Sahn, David E. ed. 1989a. Seasonal Variability in Third World Agriculture: The Consequences for Food Security. Baltimore, MD: John Hopkins University Press.

Sahn, David E. 1989b. *The Implications of Variability in Food Production for National and Household Food Security*. In Variability in Grain Yields, eds. by Jock R. Anderson and Peter B. R. Hazell. Baltimore, MD.: The John Hopkins University Press.

Sahn, David E, J. von Braun. 1987. The Relationship Between Food Production and Consumption Variability: Policy Implications for Devolving Countries. *Journal of Agricultural Economics*, 38(2): 315-27.

Sandmo, Agnar. 1971. On the Theory of the Competitive Firm Under Price Uncertainty. *The American Economic Review*, 71(1): 65-73.

Schultz, Theodore W. 1964. Transforming Traditional Agriculture. New Haven: Yale University Press.

Sen, Amartya. 1976. Poverty: An Ordinal Approach to Measurement. *Econometrica.* 44(2): 219-31.

_____. 1980. *Levels of Poverty Policy and Change.* World Bank Staff Working Paper no. 401.

_____. 1981. Poverty and Famines an Essay on Entailment and Deprivation. Clarendon Press, Oxford, U.K.

Shahabuddin, Quazi. 1982. Farmers' Crop Growing Decisions under Uncertainty -- A Safety-First Approach. The Bangladesh Development Studies. vol. 10. no. 3.

Shahabuddin, Quazi and Stuart Mestelman. 1986. Uncertainty and Disaster - Avoidance Behavior in Peasant Farming: Evidence from Bangladesh. The Journal of Development Studies. vol.22. no. 4.

Shapouri, Shahla and Margaret Missiaen. 1990. Food Aid : Motivation and Allocation Criteria. USDA ERS Foreign Agricultural Report. no. 240.

Sharif, Mohammed. 1986. The Concept and Measurement of Subsistence: A Survey of the Literature. *World Development.* 14(5): 555-78.

Sicular. Terry. 1986. *Using a Farm-Household Model to Analyze Labor Allocation on a Chinese Collective Farm.* in Agricultural Household Models. ed. by Inderjit Singh, Lyn Squire and John Strauss. Baltimore, MD.: The John Hopkins University Press.

Singh, Inderjit, Lyn Squire, and John Strauss (SSS). 1986a. A Survey of Agricultural Household Models: Recent Findings and Policy Implication. *The World Bank Economic Review*, 1(1): 149-179

_____. eds. 1986b. Agricultural Household Models: Extensions, Applications, and Policy. Baltimore, MD.: The John Hopkins University Press.

_____. 1986c. *The Basic Model: Theory, Empirical Results, and Policy Conclusions.* in Agricultural Household Models: Extensions,

Applications, and Policy. eds by SSS. Baltimore, MD.: The John Hopkins University Press.

Song, Guoqing. 1987. *From Unified Procurement to Land Tax.* in Research on China's Food Issue. ed. by Gao Xiaomeng and Song Guoqing. Being: Economic Management Publishing House.

State Statistics Bureau of China (SSB). 1981, 1985, 1989, 1990, 1992. Zhongguo Tongji Nianjian (Chinese Statistics Yearbook). Bejing: Chinese Statistics Publishing House.

Stone, Bruce. 1988. Developments in Agricultural Technology. The China Quarterly. vol. 116: 767-822.

Strauss, John. 1982. Determinants of Food Consumption in Rural Sierra Leone. Application of the Quadratic Expenditure System to the Consumption-Leisure Component of a Household-Firm Model. *Journal of Development Economics*, 11: 327-353.

_____. 1986. *Estimating the Determinants of Food Consumption and Caloric Availability in Rural Sierra Leone.* in Agricultural Household Models. Extensions, Applications, and Policy. ed. by SSS.

Taylor, Jeffrey R. and Karen A. Hardee. 1985. Consumer Demand in China: A Statistical Factbook. U.S. Bureau of the Census: Centre for International Research, and International Statistical Programs Centre.

Timmer, Peter. 1983. Food Policy Analysis. World Bank Publication. Baltimore, MD.: The John Hopkink University Press.

Tong, Yaming. 1991. *Poverty Issues and Policies in China. The Case of Luliang District in Shanxi Province.* China Paper 91/5. National Centre for Development Studies. The Australian National University.

Tong, Zhong, Scott Rozelle, Bruce Stone, Jiang Dehua, Chen Jiyuan, and Xu Zhikang. 1992. *China's Experience with market Reform for Commercialization of Agriculture in Poor Areas.* in Commercialization in developing Countries. ed. by Joachim von Braun, Eileen Kennedy. Washington, D.C.: International Food Policy Research Institute.

Toquero, Zenaida, Bart Duff, Teresa Anden-Lacsina, and Yujiro Hayami. 1975. Marketed Surplus Functions for a Subsistence Crop: Rice in the Philippines. American Journal of Agricultural Economics. vol. 57. no. 4.

Tsakok, Esabelle. 1990. Agricultural Price Policy - A- Practitioner's Guide to Partial-Equilibrium Analysis. Ithaca: Cornell University Press.

Turnovsky, S. J., H. Shalit, and A. Schmitz. 1980. Consumer's Surplus, Price Instability, and Consumer Welfare. *Econometrica*, 48: 135-52.

Walker, Kenneth R. 1965. Planning in Chinese Agriculture Socialisation and the Private Sector 1956-1962. Chicago: Aldine Publishing Company.

Walker, Kenneth R. 1984. Food Grain Procurement and Consumption in China. Cambridge: Cambridge University Press.

Wang, Xiaoqiang and Bai Nansheng. 1987. The Poverty of Plenty. Chengdu: Sichuan Publishing House. (cited from Zhu Ling. 1992).

Wharton, Clifton R. Jr. ed. 1986. Subsistence Agriculture and Economic Development. Chicago: Aldine.

Whitehead, Ann. 1988. Distributional Effects of Cash Crop Innovation: The Perpherally Commercialized Farmers of North East Ghana. IDS Bullentin. vol. 19. no. 2.

Wiens, Thomas B. 1976. Peasant Risk Aversion and Allocative Behaviour: A Quadratic Programming Experiment. *American Journal of Agricultural Economics*, 58(2): 629-35.

_____. 1977. *Uncertainty and Factor Allocation in a Peasant Economy*. Oxford Economic Papers vol. 29, no. 1.

_____. 1982. The Microeconomics of Peasant Economy. China, 1920-1940. Garland Publishing, Inc., New York & London.

_____. 1985. *Poverty and Progress in the Huang and Huai River Basins*. in Chinese Rural Development. the Great Transformation. ed. by William L. Parish. M.E. Aharpe, Inc.

World Bank. 1985. China to the Year 2000. Washington, D.C.: The World Bank.

World Bank. 1990. The World Development Report 1990. Poverty. Washington, D.C.: The World Bank.

World Bank. 1993. China: Strategies for Reducing Poverty in the 1990s. Washington, D.C.: The World Bank.

World Food Programme (WFP). 1990. 1990 Food Aid Review.

World Health Organization (WHO). 1985. Energy and Protein Requirements. Report of a Joint FAO/WHO/UNU Expert Consultation. WHO Technical Report Series 724.

Wu, Haizhen. 1989. *The Inquiry of Reforming Marketing System of Grain Commodity During the Seventh-Five Plan in China.* in China's Marketing of Agricultural Products. ed. by The Research Group of Rural Commodity Circulation. Beijing: Publishing House of Economic Management.

Xihua Dispatches. April, 29, 1991. State to Increase Grain and Oil Prices. in *China Daily*.

Yan, Ruizhen. 1990. Zhongguo Pinkun Shanqu de Jingji Kafa yu Jishu Yinjin (The Economic Development and Technology Introduction in China's Poor Mountainous Areas). Bejing: Chinese People's University Rural Research Institute.

Yotopoulos, Pan, Lawrence Lau, and Wuu-long Lin. 1976. Microeconomic Output Supply and Factor Demand Functions in the Agriculture of the Province of Taiwan. *American Journal of Agricultural Economics*, 58: 333-40.

Zhu, Ling. 1992. Study on Poverty. Unpublished memo. The Ecionomic Research Insititute of Chinese Academy of Social Sciences.

Zweig, David. 1985. *Peasants, Ideology, and New Incentive Systems: Jiangsu Province, 1978-1981.* in Chinese Rural Development The Great Transformation. ed. by Parish. M.E. Sharpe, Inc.

ANNEX. I <u>MATHEMATICAL ANNEX</u>: <u>Agricultural Household Model</u>

A1. <u>Basic Model</u>

The Lagrangian function can be written:

(1.6) $\mathcal{L} = U(C_f, C_n, Z) + \lambda[P_f(F_f\text{-}C_f) + P_cF_c + E - P_nC_n$
$+ \mu[F(F_f, L_f, A_f)] + \phi[G(F_c, L\text{-}L_f, A\text{-}A_f)]$

Assuming there is an interior solution, the first-order conditions can be written as:

(1.7)

$$\frac{\partial \mathcal{L}}{\partial C_f} = U_f - \lambda P_f = 0$$

$$\frac{\partial \mathcal{L}}{\partial C_n} = U_n - \lambda P_n = 0$$

$$\frac{\partial \mathcal{L}}{\partial \lambda} = P_f(F_f\text{-}C_f) + P_cF_c + E - C_nP_n = 0$$

$$\frac{\partial \mathcal{L}}{\partial F_f} = \lambda P_f + \mu F_F = 0 \quad or \quad \frac{1}{\lambda}\frac{\partial \mathcal{L}}{\partial F_c} = P_f + \frac{\mu}{\lambda}F_F = 0$$

$$\frac{\partial \mathcal{L}}{\partial F_c} = \lambda P_c + \varphi G_c = 0 \quad or \quad \frac{1}{\lambda}\frac{\partial \mathcal{L}}{\partial F_c} = P_c + \frac{\varphi}{\lambda}G_c = 0$$

$$\frac{\partial \mathcal{L}}{\partial \mu} = F(F_f, L_f, A_f) = 0$$

$$\frac{\partial \mathcal{L}}{\partial \varphi} = G(F_c, \bar{L} - L_f, \bar{A} - A_f) = 0$$

$$\frac{\partial \mathcal{L}}{\partial L_f} = \mu F_L - \varphi G_L = 0 \quad or \quad \frac{1}{\lambda}\frac{\partial \mathcal{L}}{\partial L_f} = \frac{\mu}{\lambda}F_L - \frac{\varphi}{\lambda}G_L = 0$$

$$\frac{\partial \mathcal{L}}{\partial A_f} = \mu F_A - \varphi G_A = 0 \quad or \quad \frac{1}{\lambda}\frac{\partial \mathcal{L}}{\partial A_f} = \frac{\mu}{\lambda}F_A - \frac{\varphi}{\lambda}G_A = 0$$

Total differentiating 1.7, the Hessian matrix is as follows:

(1.8)

$$
\begin{bmatrix}
U_{ff} & U_{fn} & -P_f & 0 & 0 & 0 & 0 & 0 & 0 \\
U_{nf} & U_{nn} & -P_n & 0 & 0 & 0 & 0 & 0 & 0 \\
-P_f & -P_n & 0 & 0 & 0 & 0 & 0 & 0 & 0 \\
0 & 0 & 0 & \frac{\mu}{\lambda}F_{FF} & 0 & \frac{\mu}{\lambda}F_{FL} & \frac{\mu}{\lambda}F_{FA} & F_F & 0 \\
0 & 0 & 0 & 0 & \frac{\varphi}{\lambda}G_{cc} & -\frac{\varphi}{\lambda}G_{cL} & -\frac{\varphi}{\lambda}G_{cA} & 0 & -G_c \\
0 & 0 & 0 & F_F & 0 & F_L & F_A & 0 & 0 \\
0 & 0 & 0 & G_c & 0 & -G_L & G_A & 0 & 0 \\
0 & 0 & 0 & \frac{\mu}{\lambda}F_{LF} & -\frac{\varphi}{\mu}G_{Lc} & (\frac{\mu}{\lambda}F_{LL}-\frac{\varphi}{\mu}G_{LL}) & (\frac{\mu}{\lambda}F_{LA}-\frac{\varphi}{\mu}G_{LA}) & F_L & -G_L \\
0 & 0 & 0 & \frac{\mu}{\lambda}F_{AF} & -\frac{\varphi}{\mu}G_{Ac} & (\frac{\mu}{\lambda}F_{AL}-\frac{\varphi}{\mu}G_{AL}) & (\frac{\mu}{\lambda}F_{AA}-\frac{\varphi}{\mu}G_{AA}) & F_A & -G_A
\end{bmatrix}
$$

$$
\begin{bmatrix}
dC_f \\
dC_n \\
d\lambda \\
dF_f \\
dF_c \\
dL_f \\
dA_f \\
d(\frac{\mu}{\lambda}) \\
d(\frac{\varphi}{\lambda})
\end{bmatrix}
=
\begin{bmatrix}
\lambda dP_f \\
\lambda dP_n \\
\psi \\
-dP_f \\
-dP_c \\
0 \\
0 \\
0 \\
0
\end{bmatrix}
$$

where $\psi = C_n dP_n - (F_f-C_f)dP_f - dE - F_c dP_c$. (In differentiating the budget constraint, we eliminate the coefficients on dF_f and dF_c by substitutions utilizing the first-order conditions determining marginal rates of substitution for the production inputs and equating price with marginal value product, as well as the sixth and seventh equations of the Hessian. Compare Singh, Squire and Strauss, p. 74, for a similar manipulation.)

The upper left block of three equations of the Hessian matrix is the solution for commodity demand and marginal income. The lower right six equations are the output supply and input demand solutions. As the Hessian is block diagonal, the system is recursive.

A2. Introducing Quotas into the Model

The Lagrangian equation is follows:

(2.8) $\mathcal{L} = U(C_f, C_n, Z) + \lambda(Q_f P_q + P_f(F_f - Q_f - (C_f - R_r))) + E + F_c P_c - P_r R_r - P_n C_n)$
$+ \mu[F(F_f, L_f, A_f)] + \phi[G(F_c, L-L_f, A-A_f)] + \theta[R_r - (F_f - Q_f) + T(Z)]$

The first-order conditions are:
(2.9)

$$\frac{\partial\mathcal{L}}{\partial C_f} = U_f - \lambda P_f = 0$$

$$\frac{\partial\mathcal{L}}{\partial C_n} = U_n - \lambda P_n = 0$$

$$\frac{\partial\mathcal{L}}{\partial \lambda} = Q_f P_q + P_f(F_f - Q_f - (C_f - R_r)) + F_c P_c - P_r R_r - P_n C_n = 0$$

$$\frac{\partial\mathcal{L}}{\partial F_f} = \lambda P_f + \mu F_F - \theta = 0 \quad or \quad \frac{1}{\lambda}\frac{\partial\mathcal{L}}{\partial F_f} = P_f + \frac{\mu}{\lambda}F_F - \frac{\theta}{\lambda} = 0$$

$$\frac{\partial\mathcal{L}}{\partial F_c} = \lambda P_c + \varphi G_c = 0 \quad or \quad \frac{1}{\lambda}\frac{\partial\mathcal{L}}{\partial F_c} = P_c + \frac{\varphi}{\lambda}G_c = 0$$

$$\frac{\partial\mathcal{L}}{\partial \mu} = F(F_f, L_f, A_f) = 0$$

$$\frac{\partial\mathcal{L}}{\partial \varphi} = G(F_c, \bar{L} - L_f, \bar{A} - A_f) = 0$$

$$\frac{\partial\mathcal{L}}{\partial L_f} = \mu F_L - \varphi G_L = 0 \quad or \quad \frac{1}{\lambda}\frac{\partial\mathcal{L}}{\partial L_f} = \frac{\mu}{\lambda}F_L - \frac{\varphi}{\lambda}G_L = 0$$

$$\frac{\partial\mathcal{L}}{\partial A_f} = \mu F_A - \varphi G_A = 0 \quad or \quad \frac{1}{\lambda}\frac{\partial\mathcal{L}}{\partial A_f} = \frac{\mu}{\lambda}F_A - \frac{\varphi}{\lambda}G_A = 0$$

$$\frac{\partial \mathcal{L}}{\partial \theta} = R_r - [F_f - Q_f) + T(Z) = 0$$

$$\frac{\partial \mathcal{L}}{\partial R} = \lambda(P_f - P_r) + \theta = 0 \quad or \quad \frac{1}{\lambda}\frac{\partial \mathcal{L}}{\partial R} = P_f - P_r + \frac{\theta}{\lambda} = 0$$

Totally differentiating (2.8), the Hessian matrix is follows:

(2.10)

$$
\begin{bmatrix}
U_{ff} & U_{fn} & -P_f & 0 & 0 & 0 & 0 & 0 & 0 & 0 & 0 \\
U_{nf} & U_{nn} & -P_n & 0 & 0 & 0 & 0 & 0 & 0 & 0 & 0 \\
-P_f & -P_n & 0 & 0 & 0 & 0 & 0 & 0 & 0 & 0 & 0 \\
0 & 0 & 0 & \frac{\mu}{\lambda}F_{FF} & 0 & \frac{\mu}{\lambda}F_{FL} & \frac{\mu}{\lambda}F_{FA} & F_F & 0 & 0 & 0 \\
0 & 0 & 0 & 0 & \frac{\varphi}{\lambda}G_{cc} & -\frac{\varphi}{\lambda}G_{cL} & -\frac{\varphi}{\lambda}G_{cA} & 0 & -G_c & 0 & 0 \\
0 & 0 & 0 & F_F & 0 & F_L & F_A & 0 & 0 & 0 & 0 \\
0 & 0 & 0 & 0 & G_c & -G_L & G_A & 0 & 0 & 0 & 0 \\
0 & 0 & 0 & \frac{\mu}{\lambda}F_{LF} & -\frac{\varphi}{\mu}G_{Lc} & (\frac{\mu}{\lambda}F_{LL}-\frac{\varphi}{\mu}G_{LL}) & (\frac{\mu}{\lambda}F_{LA}-\frac{\varphi}{\mu}G_{LA}) & F_L & -G_L & 0 & 0 \\
0 & 0 & 0 & \frac{\mu}{\lambda}F_{AF} & -\frac{\varphi}{\mu}G_{Ac} & (\frac{\mu}{\lambda}F_{AL}-\frac{\varphi}{\mu}G_{AL}) & (\frac{\mu}{\lambda}F_{AA}-\frac{\varphi}{\mu}G_{AA}) & F_A & -G_A & 0 & 0 \\
0 & 0 & 0 & -F_F & 0 & -F_L & F_A & 0 & 0 & 1 & 0 \\
0 & 0 & 0 & 0 & 0 & 0 & 0 & 0 & 0 & 0 & 1
\end{bmatrix}
$$

$$
\begin{bmatrix}
dC_f \\
dC_n \\
d\lambda \\
dF_f \\
dF_c \\
dL_f \\
dA_f \\
d(\frac{\mu}{\lambda}) \\
d(\frac{\varphi}{\lambda}) \\
dR_r \\
d(\frac{\theta}{\lambda})
\end{bmatrix}
=
\begin{bmatrix}
\lambda dP_f \\
\lambda dP_n \\
\psi \\
-dP_f \\
-dP_c \\
0 \\
0 \\
0 \\
0 \\
0 \\
dP_r - dP_f
\end{bmatrix}
$$

where $\psi = \quad -(P_q-P_f)dQ_f - (dP_f-dP_r)Q_f + (dP_f-dP_r)R_r - (F_f-C_f)dP_f - F_c dP_c + C_n dP_n - dE$

(Again, by manipulation of the last row of the Hessian and several of the first-order conditions, it can be shown that $p_f dF_f + p_c dF_c = (p_f-p_r)dR$, which eliminates the extra terms from row three of the Hessian.) The Hessian remains block diagonal, so the separability property still holds if there is an internal solution.

A3. Introducing Labor Market and Labor-Leisure Choice

The Lagrangian equation is:

(3.2) $\mathcal{L} = U(C_f, C_n, C_l) + \lambda[P_f(F_f - C_f) \pm F_c P_c + w(T - C_l - L_f - L_c) - P_n C_n] + \mu[F(F_f, L_f, A_f)] + \phi[G(F_c, L_c, A-A_f]$

The first-order conditions are:

(3.3) $\dfrac{\partial \mathcal{L}}{\partial C_f} = U_f - \lambda P_f = 0$

$\dfrac{\partial \mathcal{L}}{\partial C_n} = U_n - \lambda P_n = 0$

$\dfrac{\partial \mathcal{L}}{\partial C_l} = U_l - \lambda w = 0$

$\dfrac{\partial \mathcal{L}}{\partial \lambda} = P_f(F_f - C_f) + F_c P_c - P_n C_n + w(T - C_l - L_f - L_c) = 0$

$\dfrac{\partial \mathcal{L}}{\partial F_f} = \lambda P_f + \mu F_F = 0 \quad or \quad \dfrac{1}{\lambda}\dfrac{\partial \mathcal{L}}{\partial F_f} = P_f + \dfrac{\mu}{\lambda}F_F = 0$

$\dfrac{\partial \mathcal{L}}{\partial F_c} = \lambda P_c + \varphi G_c = 0 \quad or \quad \dfrac{1}{\lambda}\dfrac{\partial \mathcal{L}}{\partial F_c} = P_c + \dfrac{\varphi}{\lambda}G_c = 0$

$\dfrac{\partial \mathcal{L}}{\partial \mu} = F(F_f, L_f, A_f) = 0$

$\dfrac{\partial \mathcal{L}}{\partial \varphi} = G(F_c, L_c, \bar{A} - A_f) = 0$

$\dfrac{\partial \mathcal{L}}{\partial L_f} = -\lambda w + \mu F_L = 0 \quad or \quad \dfrac{1}{\lambda}\dfrac{\partial \mathcal{L}}{\partial L_f} = \dfrac{\mu}{\lambda}F_L - w = 0$

$\dfrac{\partial \mathcal{L}}{\partial L_c} = -\lambda w + \varphi G_L = 0 \quad or \quad \dfrac{1}{\lambda}\dfrac{\partial \mathcal{L}}{\partial L_c} = \dfrac{\varphi}{\lambda}G_L - w = 0$

$\dfrac{\partial \mathcal{L}}{\partial A_f} = \mu F_A - \varphi G_A = 0 \quad or \quad \dfrac{1}{\lambda}\dfrac{\partial \mathcal{L}}{\partial A_f} = \dfrac{\mu}{\lambda}F_A - \dfrac{\varphi}{\lambda}G_A = 0$

Since both the labor market and consumption of leisure are introduced into the model, the second-order conditions are changed as follows:

(3.4)

$$
\begin{pmatrix}
U_{ff} & U_{fn} & U_{fl} & -P_f & 0 & 0 & 0 & 0 & 0 & 0 & 0 \\
U_{nf} & U_{nn} & U_{nl} & -P_n & 0 & 0 & 0 & 0 & 0 & 0 & 0 \\
U_{lf} & U_{ln} & U_{ll} & -w & 0 & 0 & 0 & 0 & 0 & 0 & 0 \\
-P_f & -P_n & -w & 0 & 0 & 0 & 0 & 0 & 0 & 0 & 0 \\
0 & 0 & 0 & 0 & \dfrac{\mu}{\lambda}F_{FF} & \dfrac{\mu}{\lambda}F_{FL} & \dfrac{\mu}{\lambda}F_{FA} & 0 & 0 & F_F & 0 \\
0 & 0 & 0 & 0 & 0 & 0 & \dfrac{\varphi}{\lambda}G_{cA} & \dfrac{\varphi}{\lambda}G_{cc} & -\dfrac{\varphi}{\lambda}G_{cL} & 0 & -G_c \\
0 & 0 & 0 & 0 & F_F & F_L & F_A & 0 & 0 & 0 & 0 \\
0 & 0 & 0 & 0 & 0 & 0 & G_A & G_c & G_L & 0 & 0 \\
0 & 0 & 0 & 0 & \dfrac{\mu}{\lambda}F_{LF} & \dfrac{\mu}{\lambda}F_{LL} & \dfrac{\mu}{\lambda}F_{LA} & 0 & 0 & F_L & 0 \\
0 & 0 & 0 & 0 & 0 & 0 & \dfrac{\varphi}{\lambda}G_{LA} & \dfrac{\varphi}{\lambda}G_{Lc} & \dfrac{\varphi}{\lambda}G_{LL} & 0 & G_L \\
0 & 0 & 0 & 0 & \dfrac{\mu}{\lambda}F_{AF} & \dfrac{\mu}{\lambda}F_{AL} & \left(\dfrac{\mu}{\lambda}F_{AA}-\dfrac{\varphi}{\lambda}G_{AA}\right) & -\dfrac{\varphi}{\lambda}G_{Ac} & -\dfrac{\varphi}{\lambda}G_{AL} & F_A & G_A
\end{pmatrix}
$$

$$
\begin{pmatrix}
dC_f \\
dC_n \\
dC_t \\
d\lambda \\
dF_f \\
dL_f \\
dA_f \\
dF_c \\
dL_c \\
d\left(\dfrac{\mu}{\lambda}\right) \\
d\left(\dfrac{\varphi}{\lambda}\right)
\end{pmatrix}
=
\begin{pmatrix}
\lambda dP_f \\
\lambda dP_n \\
\lambda dw \\
\psi \\
-dP_f \\
-dP_c \\
0 \\
0 \\
dw \\
dw \\
0
\end{pmatrix}
$$

where $\psi =$ $\quad C_n dP_n - (F_f-C_f)dP_f - dE - F_c dP_c - (T-C_l-L_f L_c)dw$

A5. Introducing Risk and Risk Aversion

V_y can be approximated using a Taylor series expansion around average prices $\bar{P}_f$ and $\bar{P}_c$ and income $\bar{y}$:

(5.5) $\quad V_y \approx \bar{V}_y + \sum_{k=1}^{M} \bar{V}_{yp_k}(P_k - \bar{P}_k) + \bar{V}_{yy}(Y - \bar{Y})$

where $\bar{V}_y$ is the evaluation of V_y at mean income and prices, and k here represents only two commodities, food and non-food.

Roy's identity is:

$V_{p_i} = - V_y q_i$ where q_i is the Marshallian demand for good i

Differentiating Roy's identity with respect to income, y, and the p_i, and substituting into (5.5) for V_{yy} and V_{yp}, the equation becomes:

$V_y \approx \bar{V}_y [1 - \sum_{k=1}^{M} \bar{q}_k (\frac{\eta_k}{y} - \frac{\psi}{y})(p_k - \bar{p}_k) - \frac{\psi}{y}(y - \bar{y})]$

where $\Psi = -\bar{y}\bar{V}_{yy} / \bar{V}_y$ is the coefficient of relative risk aversion with respect to income variability and q_k and η_k are quantity consumed and income elasticity of consumption, all at average price and income, $(\bar{p}, \bar{y})$. Multiplying by π_i and taking expectations, the equation becomes

(5.6) $E[V_y \pi_i] \approx \bar{V}_y \{E[\pi_i] - \sum_{k=1}^{M} s_k (\eta_k - \psi) E[\pi_i(\frac{p_k}{p_k} - 1)] - \psi E[\pi_i(\frac{y}{y}-1)]\}$

where s_k is the consumption share of good k at average prices and income $\bar{p}_k \bar{q}_k / \bar{y}$.

Substituting (5.6) into (5.4), dividing by $\bar{V}_y$ and by numerary $E[\pi_n]$:

$$(m_i - m_j)(1 + \psi) \qquad (P)$$

$$(5.7) \quad + \sum_{k=1}^{M} CV_{p_i}(m_j \rho_{\pi_i p_i} CV_{\pi_i} - m_j \rho \pi_j p_k CV_{\pi_i}) s_k(\eta_k - \psi) \quad (Q)$$

$$-\psi \frac{E[(\pi_i - \pi_j)y]}{yE[\pi_n]} \approx 0 \qquad (X)$$

where $m_i = E[\pi_i]/E[\pi_n]$, CV is the coefficient of variation, and ρ is the coefficient of correlation. The choice of numerary makes it dimension-free and therefore homogenous of degree zero in all prices and revenues (Fafchamps). The equation must hold for all interior i and j.

To solve for the optimal crop portfolio, define:

$$a_i = \frac{A_i}{A} \quad \text{and write farm income per hectare as} \quad \frac{y}{A} = \sum_{i=1}^{N} a_i \pi_i . \quad \text{Note that}$$

$$\sum_{i=1}^{N} a_i = 1 \quad and \quad \sum_{i=1}^{N} a_i m_i = \sum_{i=1}^{N} a_i \frac{E[\pi_i]}{E[\pi_n]} . \quad \text{Ignoring terms (P) and (Q) in}$$

(5.7) and using these relations to manipulate (X), consolidating terms using the definitions of the coefficients of variation and correlation CV and ρ , we derive a system of N linear equations (including the requirement that crop proportions sum to one) in N unknowns.

In our model, M (consumption goods) and N (produced crops) both equal two, and the interior solution for the optimal proportion of acreage in the food crop f is[17]:

$$(5.8) \quad A_f^* \approx \frac{-(P+Q)-\psi s}{(m-1)(P+Q)+\psi T}$$

where $T = CV_{\pi_c}^2 + m_f^2 CV_{\pi_f}^2 + (1-m_f)^2 - 2m_f \rho_{\pi_c \pi_f} CV_{\pi_c} CV_{\pi_f}$

$$S = m \rho_{\pi_c \pi_f} CV_{\pi_c} CV_{\pi_f} - CV_{\pi_c}^2 + m_f - 1$$

---

[17] Sign errors appear in the last terms of the numerator and denominator of Fafchamps' corresponding equation (3).

ANNEX II. RURAL PER CAPITA NUTRITIONAL STANDARD IN 1988

	Unprocessed			Processed			Vegeta-bles	Edible oil	Red meat	Poul-try	Eggs	Fish	Nutrition	
	Rice	Wheat	Corn	Rice	Wheat	Corn							Energy	Protein
Calories/kg				3660	3500	3620	262	8840	3596	1250	1450	630	(KCal/day)	(gm/day)
Protein/kg				64	113	90	16		59	101	115	89		
Conversion to Processed Wt.				67%	90%	91%								
Consumption per capita in kilograms:														
Income quintile:														
I	88	84	42	59	76	38	94	1.38	5.10	0.32	1.20	0.20	1,853	49
II	128	81	32	86	73	29	111	1.66	10.10	0.49	1.50	0.30	2,075	52
III	157	74	24	105	67	22	122	1.94	11.10	0.57	1.90	0.50	2,164	52
IV	157	72	23	105	65	21	136	3.33	15.10	0.73	4.30	0.90	2,232	54
V	175	68	22	117	61	20	223	2.18	37.20	1.54	3.20	0.80	2,560	62
ORBA /1	169	72	30	113	65	27	122	2.21	9.38	0.63	2.13	0.77	2,273	55
Border area	195	34	57	131	31	52	134	1.73	15.85	2.94	1.31	0.62	2,429	55
Minority area	132	21	50	88	19	46	129	1.09	12.52	1.14	1.23	0.18	1,771	41
Poor area	125	70	45	84	63	41	111	1.45	13.00	0.54	1.18	0.22	2,100	52
Other	142	82	23	95	74	21	146	1.98	17.10	0.81	2.30	0.60	2,203	55
Income quintile														
(within poor area):														67

ANNEX.III The Determination of Poverty Line

Population Poverty Line. As mentioned above, the poverty line was set at 200 yuan per capita in 1985. Although precise information on how this figure was arrived at is not available, it appears consistent with a detailed re-estimate based on 1988 survey data, as shown below.

The population poverty line was calculated as the value of consumption of foods meeting minimum nutritional requirements plus expenditures on basic requirements of other goods and services. Both in computing net per capita incomes and in determining a poverty line, it has been customary to apply quota (or, post-1985, contract) prices in valuing self-produced items of consumption.

In order to estimate the cost of a food basket providing a daily caloric intake of 2,400 KCal, the actual consumption quantities of various foods by the Chinese rural population with daily caloric intake below 2,400 KCal. were estimated from the 60,000 household annual survey taken by the State Statistics Bureau. Average prices for each item were estimated as weighted average of quota (contract) and market prices, the weights being the proportions self-produced and purchased respectively (RGCPA, 1989). The results are shown in Table AIII.1.

Table AIII.1. Expenditure on Food Per Capita Per Year. 1988

Items	Consumption (kg) Q_i	Average Price (yuan/kg) P_i	Value (yuan) $Q_i P_i$
Grains	194.40	0.35	68.87
Vegetable	100.90	0.24	23.96
Edible Oil	2.30	2.90	6.78
Pork	8.27	3.95	32.67
Beef & Mutton	0.53	4.05	2.14
Milk	0.22	0.62	0.14
Poultry	0.05	4.05	0.20
Eggs	1.68	3.36	5.64
Fish	1.13	3.02	3.41
Sugar	1.45	2.24	3.25
Fruit	4.04	0.93	3.73
Total	NA	NA	150.79

Source: RGCPA, 1989.

Since the average caloric value of this food basket is 2,152 KCal., it is necessary to inflate the consumption and expenditure figures by the ratio 2,400/2,152 to obtain the approximate value of a 2,400 KCal. food basket, which is thus 168.1 yuan.

This is approximately the same as the average expenditure on food (165.2 yuan) by that group of households with per capita incomes under 300 yuan. It is therefore convenient to take the average expenditures of such households on clothing and other daily necessities -- 49.5 yuan -- and subtract from this expenditures on luxuries (6.8 yuan), to obtain an estimate of minimum required expenditures on clothing and other daily necessities for inclusion in the poverty line (42.7 yuan).

Currently the average living area of the rural population is 16.58 sq. m. In 1978-88, housing represented 11.9% of total rural expenditure on average, or 56.7 yuan based on 1988 total incomes. Adjusting this proportionately to the assumed minimum standard of 9 sq. m., 56.72 x 9/16.58 = 30.8 yuan. However, this figure also reflects an average quality of housing, whereas housing in poor areas is relatively lower quality and unit value. In 1987, the average value of a room in rural areas was 593 yuan, but it was 318 yuan for those whose net income was under 300 yuan. This ratio is used to adjust for quality, so that the housing expenditure reflected in the poverty line becomes .604 x 30.8 = 18.6 yuan.

Expenditure on transportation, fuel, medical care, education, and entertainment totalled 30.3 yuan, or 11.5% of total expenditure, for the rural population with income under 300 yuan.

Thus the poverty line, based on 1988 data, is the sum of:

Food	168.1 yuan
Daily Use Goods	42.7
Housing	18.6
Other Services	30.3
Total	259.7 yuan

This poverty line is not necessarily comparable to the 200 yuan criteria set in 1986 on the basis of 1985 data. However, adjustment of the 200 yuan figure to 1988 prices based on the rate of inflation (price index of consumer goods) would give a 267 yuan figure for 1988, quite similar to the above.

The poverty line should be regularly adjusted due to the inflation. The share of self-produced consumption was calculated using administered prices prior to 1985, but after 1985 using market average prices. Thus the adjustment formula should be (Zhu, 1992):

$$G = (X_1 + X_2)P_sF + (X_1 + X_2)P_m(1 - F)$$

$$G = (X_1 + X_2)P_sF + (X_1 + X_2)P_m(1 - F)$$

where X_1 expenditure on food,
            X_2 expenditure on other consumer gods and services,
            P_s price index for self-produced goods,
            P_m price index for market purchase goods, and
            F   share of consumption of self-produced (Zhu. 1992).

Household Poverty Line. Determining a household poverty line is <u>not</u> simply a matter of multiplying the population poverty line by the family size, as there are "economies of scale" in household consumption. That is, the consumption coefficient (ratio of expenditure to net income) diminishes with increased household size. Measured relative to the consumption coefficient of a "typical" five person rural household, Table AIII.2 indicates how the coefficient varies with household size:

Table AIII.2. The Influence of Family Size on Consumption Level

# of Family Member(s)	1 Person	2-3 Persons	4-6 Persons	Above 7
Index (5 Person Family = 100)	106.8	102.72	100.11	96.76

Source: RGCPA, 1989.

Printed and bound by CPI Group (UK) Ltd, Croydon, CR0 4YY

08/05/2025

01864494-0003